The International Garlic Festival Cookbook

A recipe collection from garlic lovers around the world.

Compiled and written by Caryl Simpson

Design & Illustration: Caryl Simpson
Cover Art & Design: Carlos Munoz
Typeset by Sheryl Cathers

Printed in the United States of America

Third Printing

To order directly from the publisher write :
Intl. Garlic FestivalCookbook,
P.O. BX 1145 , Gilroy , Ca. 95021 or call 1 (888) GARLICFEST

GOURMET GOLD PRESS
GILROY, CALIFORNIA

*T*his book is dedicated to garlic lovers everywhere.

A special thanks goes to the talented friends, customers, fellow cooks & chefs and staff who contributed to this project. I would also like to thank Sheryl Cathers, who typeset, (and re-typeset), this book and Huck Hagenbuch who contributed to and helped edit it.
I am filled with thankfulness for my unique, and sometimes strange, family. I would like to thank Tom, who for 14 years, has been a supportive and loving partner, and my daughter, Heather, who has read, and read, and read and helped get this, finally, to the printer.

Message to my fellow cooks and garlic lovers.

This cookbook was meant to be used often in the kitchen. If you're like me you scribble little notes to yourself or write additional favorite recipes in the margins of your cookbooks or on little scraps of paper which you can never find again. Therefore, scattered throughout this book you will find boxes reserved for your own favorite recipes or notes.

Rx: Use every day to keep the vampires away!

Happy cooking!

Caryl Simpson

"Tomatoes and oregano make it Italian; wine and tarragon make it French; sour cream makes it Russian; lemon and cinnamon make it Greek; soy sauce makes it Chinese; **GARLIC MAKES IT GOOD!!!**"

Them Garlic Gummers

How 'bout them garlic gummers
  Ain't they funny guys?
Eatin' garlic in they soup.
  Puttin' garlic in they pies.
Eatin' it cooked
  Eatin' it raw
Eatin' that garlic,
  Suits they craw.

How 'bout them garlic gummers
  Goin 'outa they mind,
Runnin' round shoutin'
  "It's garlic gummin' time."
Them hot breath garlic gummers
  From north and south,
Stickin' them garlic cloves
  In they mouths.

How to be a garlic gummer?
  Don't try to shun it
Get yourself a garlic clove,
  Rare back and gum it!

By Tom Reed

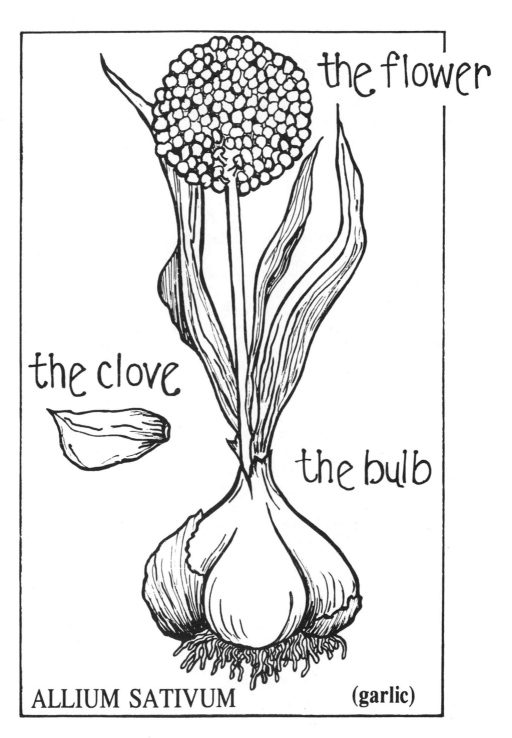

the flower

the clove

the bulb

ALLIUM SATIVUM   (garlic)

TABLE OF CONTENTS

Foreword

Garlic; Fact & Fancy
Science, medicine, and garlic.

Smell it like it is
Cooking & growing tips

Clove Encounters
Appetizers

Vampire's Bane
Soups and Salads

The Stinking Rose
Side dishes, vegetables, bread, miscellaneous

The Big Bulb
Main dishes, meats, poultry, seafood, pasta

Braised Rabbit	125
Mesquite Texas Grill	128
Veal Burt & Ernie	130
Pork with Garlic, Peppers & Balsamic Vinegar	131
Squid Stuffed with Garlic, Spinach, Feta Cheese & Rice	133
Linguini with Scallops & Herb Cream	134
Garlic Festival Chili	135
Garlic Blesssed Game Hens (Smoked)	136

Libations
Yes! You read right! Drinks!

Gartini	138
Garli Mary	138
Onion's Garlic Shooter	139
Shari Taylor's Mother's Garlic Morning Eye Opener	140
Vegetable Garlic Cocktail	140
Cincinnati Garlic Shooter	142

Fid- Aulx (Fid - o)
(Aulx; Archaic French for garlic)
Dogs like garlic too!

Heather's Garlicky Dog Biscuits	145

FOREWORD

May 16, 1993

What a stinking job, writing a foreword to a
Garlic cookbook. Many books have a FOREword;
have you ever seen a BACKword (or nautically,
would it be an AFTword?)? Who in their right nose
knows?

Despite the stinkiness of the task, it's an
honor to present a few vaporous thoughts about
garlic and its ubiquitous influence on the world and
its atmosphere. Pilots flying over Gilroy, California,
"Garlic Capital of the World", report pungent fumes
to great heights during the harvest season.
However, no astronauts have yet reported such
eminent emanations beyond the immediate
atmosphere.

Be that as it may, garlic has always
enjoyed a high level of honor and utility throughout
the ages. It transcends reality. Garlic dwells
deeply within mythological and historical lore,
from the Balkans to China and across the ocean to
the Americas. Truly, garlic enjoys world-wide
recognition, whether olfactor-ally, to coin a word, or
agriculturally, or both.

The International Garlic Festival Cookbook
is not a historical review of garlic, nor does it deal
with the mythology of garlic. We assume you know
about garlic, and enjoy it without a lot of
intellectual baggage encumbering your
enjoyment. You are, we think, merely intent on
using it more or better. That's what brought about
the International Garlic Festival Cookbook.

10

If you are a late-comer to garlic, you may want to learn a tad more about it, so you may want to explore one of the many festivals celebrating the Stinking Rose, as it has come to be known, throughout America and the world. Perhaps the largest and best-known is the festival in Gilroy, which has been featured on morning TV shows for years. Lesser known but similar festivals are held throughout the nation, such as the "Glutton for Garlic" festival in Hartford, CT; the Northwest Garlic Festival, in Ocean Park, Washington; or two odiferous festivals in Arizona.

Elsewhere in the U. S., garlic reeks with success in Arizona, Colorado, Virginia, Washington and of course, California. Over the sea, Takko Machi, Japan is Gilroy's sister city in garlic. Arleux, France, also hosts a garlic festival. So, who knows (the nose knows!)? If your timing is right, your global travels can take you on an unending celebration of the stinking rose.

Take some time at home to smell the roses, or at least the stinking rose. The recipes in this cookbook have been collected from all over the world. They represent some of the best cooking ideas using garlic that have been developed by gourmet chefs and amateurs alike. Through the years, recreational cooking assumes an ever-larger role in our lives. We stay home more, entertain our friends and families and discover new delights as we experiment with gourmet cooking that is affordable to all.

If dining out is more to your liking, there are restaurants springing up throughout the country that are dedicated to garlic cuisine. One of the first is the Stinking Rose in San Francisco. They have generously shared some of their favorite recipes with the International Garlic Festival Cookbook.

Newly opened as the International Garlic Festival Cookbook goes to press is the Garlic Cafe in Las Vegas, Nevada. They, too, have contributed recipes for your enjoyment. Next time Lady Luck takes you there, be sure to pay them a visit.

Throughout recipes in this book are references to a variety of specific products such as Garli Garni™, sun dried tomatoes and other products that have evolved through the years to enhance gourmet enjoyment. A section at the back of the book offers a complete listing of these products, and how to obtain them.

Garlic (defined as an herb, and not, as many think, as a vegetable), is grown in the U. S., predominately in California. Gilroy companies process more than half of the fresh and processed garlic supplied to world markets. The town also hosts about 150,000 visitors annually at their three-day festival, on the last weekend of July each year.

No matter which of the many uses to which you put this cookbook, use it knowing that your appreciation of garlic is shared universally. Garlic is the common thread linking virtually every cuisine and culture throughout the world. Garlic is as modern as it is ancient. Whereas our ancestors only knew that garlic was good for them, modern science and medicine are just now discovering why it's so good for us. We often get the notion that something that tastes so good has to be bad for us. Garlic refutes this wives' tale. It is good!

F.H. "Huck" Hagenbuch

12

GARLIC:
FACT & FANCY

Science, medicine, and garlic.

A Clove A Day?

Records of garlic's medicinal and therapeutic value date back nearly 4000 years to an Egyptian scroll prescribing a garlic poultice to heal skin ulcers. Roman gladiators ate garlic to increase their strength and stamina.

However, garlic was long considered just an ingredient in the anecdotes of folk medicine. Not so today. Today garlic is the subject of intense medical research with more than a thousand scientific papers having been published about the various aspects of Allium. Many important findings have been made by modern science concerning the potential benefits of garlic on allergies, high blood pressure, cancer, viral and fungal infections, stress, cardiovascular disease, and even immune deficiency diseases.

In the not so distant past, Albert Schweitzer used garlic to treat dysentery and cholera in Africa. During both World War I and World War II garlic was used to fight infection and gangrene in the absence of modern antibiotics.

It is becoming clear...GARLIC IS GOOD FOR YOU! What a relief to find something that is not only delicious, but healthy too; something you won't have to give up eating.

This book, however, is not devoted to the therapeutic and medicinal uses of the "stinking rose". It is devoted to those who like garlic in anything and everything and are consuming it in ever-greater quantities.

None-the-less, for those interested in pursuing more than the flavor of garlic, we have included a reading list at the end of this section.

ATTENTION
MOMS TO BE!!!

Some fascinating new information to impart concerning garlic and nursing mothers.....
According to a recent study conducted at Monell Chemical Senses Center in Philadelphia, Pennsylvania, babies like the flavor of garlic. Researchers found that when nursing mothers ate garlic, it had a marked effect upon the aroma of their milk. This was most pronounced when the mothers ate the garlic two hours before feeding time. The babies responded positively; they nursed for longer periods of time, and drank more.

Larry Stites
Gilroy, CA

GARLIC TEA

Add several chopped cloves of garlic to 1/2 C. of boiling water and let steep for 6 - 8 hours. Gargle for a sore throat, or swallow to ease flu symptoms.

GARLIC COUGH SYRUP

Add 1 pound of sliced garlic to 1 qt. of boiling water, and let steep for 12 hours. Add sugar or honey and vinegar boiled with caraway and fennel seeds, until the mixture reaches the consistency of syrup.

GARLIC OIL

Mix a small amount of olive oil with a slice of garlic, heat, and strain. Use a few drops of the warm oil to soothe an ear ache.

READING LIST

° Binding, G.J. About Garlic; The Supreme Herbal
    Remedy. 1981. Thorsons Publishers
    Limited. Wellingtom, Northamptonshire.

° Lau, Benjamin; M.D., PhD. Garlic for Health.
    1988. Lotus Light Publications. P.O. Box 2,
    Welmont, WI 53192

° Tulder, S. and Blackwood, J. Garlic: Nature's
    Original Remedy. 1991. Healing Arts
    Press. One Park Street, Rochester, Vermont
    05767

° The Miracle of Garlic and Vinegar. 1990. Globe
    Communications Corp. Boca Raton, Florida.

SMELL IT LIKE IT IS!

Cooking and growing tips.

COOKING TIPS

Garlic has always inspired intense passions, from scorn to adulation. The scorn is from those who have experienced it badly handled, poorly cooked, in too great a quantity. This scorn is totally unjustified. Properly handled, garlic is sweet and aromatic; completely devoid of antisocial attributes, revered by hungry souls and chefs alike.

Following are a few simple techniques and recipes that will illustrate the sublime side of garlic.

Choose plump, firm and round bulbs. There should be no garlic smell until the cloves are crushed or peeled. Store in a dry, airy place away from light and heat. Never store garlic in the refrigerator. Don't buy garlic that has sprouted unless you want to plant it in your garden.

To Peel: Cut off the root end of the clove, place the flat of a large knife on the clove(s) and hit lightly with your fist. The skins will come right off. Or... place garlic in the microwave for about 20 seconds to loosen the husks and make peeling easier.

Garlic adds flavor and dimension to almost any dish. The following recipes are some basics to keep on hand and will help liven up almost any meal.

ROASTED GARLIC-
TWO WAYS

Keep roasted garlic on hand to add rich and low calorie flavor to recipes. Add to pasta, soups, meats or spread on crusty bread. When garlic is roasted, it becomes soft, sweet, mild and nutty in flavor.

Number One:

4 whole (bulbs) garlic
1/4 tsp. dried thyme or oregano
1/4 C. olive oil

Heat oven to 350°. Peel off most of the papery outer skin of the heads. Slice off just the top off each head (the pointed end) exposing the flesh. Arrange in a small baking dish and drizzle with oil and sprinkle with herbs. Cover with foil and bake 30 - 60 minutes. Remove foil and cook another 10 - 15 minutes until garlic is soft. Cool before serving.

Number Two:

Peel desired number of whole garlic cloves, place in a shallow baking dish with about 1/8 inch olive oil. Roast in 350° oven until soft; about 45 minutes.

EASY GARLIC SALT

Into a shaker slice three cloves of fresh garlic. Add salt and the result is instant garlic salt with a fresh flavor. Use when a hint of garlic is desired. When the slices dry out, discard or use to season soup or sauces.

GARLIC BUTTER

Add 2-3 cloves of minced garlic to 1/2 cup soft butter or margarine. Also add minced herbs for garlic herb butter. Season steamed vegetables, baked potatoes or corn on the cob.

GARLIC MAYONNAISE

Similar to aioli, this is wonderful with vegetables, salads or as a sandwich spread.

2-3 cloves fresh garlic, minced
dash salt and cayenne pepper
1 C. regular or reduced calorie mayonnaise
1 Tbls. ea. lemon juice
1 Tbls. grated Parmesan cheese
3 Tbls. virgin olive oil
 fresh ground black pepper, to taste

Whisk together all ingredients except oil, Parmesan and pepper. When well blended, slowly whisk in the oil. Finally, stir in the Parmesan and pepper. Refrigerate.

Teresa's
Chef Angelo Gonzalez
Jackson, California

GARLIC SAUCE

3-4 Tbls. fresh garlic, chopped
2 Tbls. butter
1 C. good red wine
1 Tbls. capers, drained
4 sliced ripe black olives
1 tsp. roux (equal parts flour and butter
        creamed together)

Sauté garlic in 1 Tbls. of the butter until soft and golden, but not brown. Drain off butter and set garlic aside. Wipe out pan with a paper towel and add wine. Reduce by half. Add garlic, remaining butter, capers and olives. Stir in roux and stir over low heat until sauce is lightly thickened and flour is cooked. Use for roast meats.

Fresh Garlic Association
Barbara Kafka

GARLIC TO GO

Barbara Kafka is a writer for the New York Times, Vogue, Gourmet, and Family Circle.

30 cloves fresh garlic, smashed and peeled
3/4 C. + 2 Tbls. water
1/4 C. olive oil
1/2 tsp. kosher salt
fresh ground black pepper, to taste

Place garlic and water in a 1-1/2 quart soufflé dish. Cover tightly with microwave plastic wrap. Cook on high for about 8 minutes in microwave oven. Prick plastic to release steam. Remove from oven and uncover. Transfer to blender or processor and add oil, salt and pepper. Blend until smooth. Store tightly covered and refrigerated until used. Great to use for seasoning sauces, meats, soups, etc.

STIR FRY OIL

Combine 2 C. vegetable oil, 2 Tbls. chopped fresh ginger root, 2 dried red pepper flakes and 5 cloves sliced fresh garlic. Heat gently 5 minutes. Cool and transfer to glass jar. Cover and refrigerate.

THE GROWING BASICS

Garlic is propagated by planting individual cloves because seed is rarely produced. Garlic grows almost everywhere in the world and it will grow easily in your garden. You can grow it by itself or plant it around and among other plants. Garlic planting among other plants is usually an important component of organic gardening. Planting of garlic and sprays made of garlic will kill or repel many common pests while not harming the environment. It also has the additional benefit of providing you with garlic greens as well as fresh garlic for harvesting.

Garlic should be planted in late Autumn. In cold areas don't plant too early as cloves may begin to sprout and be killed by snow or frost. Garlic can also be planted in the spring for a late crop.

Cloves should be planted pointed end up about 2 inches below the earth. They should be spaced 8-10 inches apart with 12 inches between rows. Garlic likes a sunny location with good, well - worked soil.

An organic spray can be made by combining fresh garlic (about 3 oz.) in a food processor with water (1 pint) and a little oil. Allow the mixture to sit for 24 hours. Then strain and add 1/4 oz. of liquid Palmolive soap and dilute 1/20 and apply as a spray to plants. A commercial organic garlic spray is also now available. (See sources at back of book).

HOW TO GROW GARLIC

Garlic is planted in the fall or early spring in areas with temperate climates. In other areas it can be planted in large pots or planters in a greenhouse.

Plant single cloves one to three inches apart just below the surface of the soil in beds six to eight inches high. Fertilize and keep moist until first signs of maturity. **A**s garlic approaches maturity, stop watering and allow soil to dry out for harvesting. Garlic is ready to harvest when tops become dry and bend to the ground.

Place garlic on the ground to dry in the sun

Cover them with the clipped off tops to protect them from sunburn.

CLOVE
ENCOUNTERS

Appetizers

Garlic Festival Catering Co.
Gilroy, California

GARLICKY CHEESE, PEPPER & OLIVE KABOBS

1 lb. (total) mild cheeses (of choice) cut into
    bite size cubes
1 red, 1 yellow and 1 green bell pepper roasted, peeled
    and cut into thick strips
1/2-1 lb. pitted olives
1/2 C. virgin olive oil
4 cloves garlic, minced
3 Tbls. white wine vinegar
1 tsp. each; oregano, basil, thyme; finely chopped
salt and cracked pepper

    In a sealable plastic container combine the
garlic, oil, vinegar, herbs, salt, pepper & mix well.
Place cheese, peppers and olives in bowl and toss
gently to coat. Seal and marinate overnight turning
occasionally to coat. To serve, thread on small skewers
or toothpicks. Optional: marinated sun dried tomato
halves, artichoke hearts.

    To roast peppers: Poke holes in peppers with
tines of fork to let steam escape. Place over hot coals or
gas flame on burner or under broiler flame and roast
until charred evenly all around. Slice open and spread
flat. Scrape out seeds, then turn over and scrape off
charred skin.

WHOLE ROASTED GARLIC

When whole garlic bulbs are roasted, the cloves become sweet, mild and buttery...A sublime compliment to roast meat; or serve spread on crusty bread or as part of an appetizer tray.

Whole firm bulbs of garlic
fresh or dried thyme
olive oil

Heat oven to 350° to 375°. Peel off most of the papery outer skin of the garlic. Cut off just the tips of the pointed end of the bulb just exposing the cloves. Arrange in a baking dish and drizzle with olive oil and sprinkle with thyme. Cover with foil and bake for 30 - 60 minutes. Uncover and cook an additional 15 minutes or until the cloves are soft. Cool slightly and serve. Separate cloves and squeeze each out. Create an eye-catching and delicious antipasto tray with baked heads of garlic, a variety of olives, sun-dried tomatoes, steamed artichokes, feta cheese, and crusty baguettes. Arrange on a large tray of colorful greens and flowers.

GARLIC STUFFED
TOMATO APPETIZERS

1 bulb baked garlic
1 Tbls. olive oil
1 6-oz. pkg. cream cheese
1 Tbls. chopped fresh basil
1 tsp. chopped oregano
30 - 35 cherry tomatoes
fresh lemon juice

       Squeeze pulp from cooled garlic cloves into a bowl. Trim tomatoes so they sit up and slice off stem end enough to scoop out inside with a small melon ball cutter. Drain tomatoes upside down on a paper towel for about 30 minutes. In a bowl or food processor whisk together cream cheese, baked garlic, lemon juice, herbs, salt and pepper (to taste) until smooth. Use a pastry bag to pipe filling into tomato shells. Garnish with slice of black olive, capers, or caviar.

DIED & GONE
TO MONTECELLI

It was while visiting Gilroy's sister city, Montecelli, in Italy that I was first introduced to this delicious concoction. It was served in a shallow bowl with a loaf of peasant bread and a bottle of wine.

1/2 C. good virgin olive oil
1/4 C. balsamic vinegar or red wine vinegar
1 Tbls. chopped fresh basil
1 tsp. - 1 Tbls. red chili flakes (depending on how much
   heat you like)
6 cloves chopped fresh garlic

Mix all ingredients in a ceramic bowl and let stand for 10 minutes. Serve in a shallow bowl and scoop up with good crusty sourdough or peasant bread.

Babbo Ganzo

Santa Fe, New Mexico

Our friend, Giovanni Scorzo, who was trained at the prestigious professional institute, Alberghio di Stato, is a chef of uncommon talent. He and his wife, Linda, opened La Bruschetta in Scottsdale, Arizona, in 1988 and quickly created a legend. They have now opened another legend in the making in Santa Fe: "Babbo Ganzo"; which means "father" in an endearing way. His knowledge of the Tuscan kitchen and its generous use of garlic or "aglio" is brought to you in the following recipes: Zuppa Di Aglio Carciofi e Patate, (pg. 72), accompanied by Giovanni's Bruschetta.

Babbo Ganzo
Giovanni Scorzo
Santa Fe, New Mexico

BRUSCHETTA

"The original garlic bread"

Tuscan country bread, four slices
extra virgin olive oil
1 garlic clove, minced
3 Roma tomatoes, diced
10 fresh basil leaves, finely chopped
salt and pepper

      Mix together garlic, tomatoes, olive oil, basil, salt and pepper. Set aside. Grill both sides of the bread. Rub one side of the bread with a garlic clove. Then add tomato mixture. Grill again for 30 seconds. Garnish with basil leaf. Buon Appetito!!!

BASIC PICKLED GARLIC & CREAM CHEESE SPREAD

cream cheese
chopped pickled garlic
fresh chopped basil
Feta cheese (optional)

      Blend ingredients together in a food processor. Serve as a spread or a dip for crackers, croustades, or vegetables. Use your imagination to create an infinite variety of dips: add chopped sun-dried tomatoes, other herbs, olives, capers, peppers, etc.

Favorite Recipe

GARLICKY DRIED TOMATO SALMON SPREAD

1 oz. dried tomatoes, chopped
1-2 Tbls. Garli Garni™ (see sources)
1/4 C. water (hot)
8 oz. cream cheese, softened
1-2 Tbls. milk
1-2 oz. smoked salmon (or trout)

    Place chopped dried tomatoes and Garli Garni™ in a small skillet with water and heat until tomatoes are softened and have absorbed the water (1-2 minutes). Place softened cream cheese in the food processor with milk and process until smooth. Add tomatoes and mix., then add smoked salmon or trout and process just until blended. Refrigerate until serving. Serve with crackers, or crisp croustades.

GRILLED MARINATED EGGPLANT

Slice eggplant 1/4 inch thick and grill for about 2 - 5 minutes on each side; cool. Marinate flat with olive oil, garlic, salt, pepper and parsley. Refrigerate overnight. Bring to room temperature to serve.

PICKLED GARLIC
BASIL DIP

1 C. sour cream
1 C. low calorie mayonnaise
1 C. chopped fresh basil
3/4 C. fresh grated Parmesan cheese
3 Tbls. chopped pickled garlic
1 Tbls. chopped marinated sun-dried tomatoes
1/2 tsp. fresh ground black pepper

      Combine all ingredients in a bowl. Refrigerate until serving time. Serve with assorted vegetables and chips.

Favorite Recipe

GARBANZO &
GARLIC SPREAD

1 can (19-oz.) garbanzo beans
4 cloves garlic
3 Tbls. lemon juice
3 Tbls. good olive oil
Salt and pepper
1/4 C. chopped Italian parsley
Black olives

        Combine all ingredients except parsley and olives in a food processor until smooth. Stir in parsley and put in serving bowl. Store in refrigerator until serving time. Garnish with chopped black olives. Serve with pita bread or crackers.

GARLICKY DEVILED EGGS

12 eggs, hard boiled and peeled
1/4 C. mayonnaise (regular or low fat)
1/4 C. sour cream
2 Tbls. Sweet & Spicy Garlic Festival® Mustard
1/4 C. pickled garlic, chopped coarsely

      Cut eggs in half and remove yolks. Mash yolks with all ingredients (except pickled garlic) until smooth. Mound filling in egg hollows and top each with about 1/2 tsp. pickled garlic.

TAKKO-MACHI
CHICKEN WINGS

chicken wings for 10 - 12 people
1-2 Tbls. fresh grated ginger
6-8 cloves garlic, minced
4 chopped green onions
2 C. soy sauce
1 C. sugar
1 C. sake
flour

     Place all ingredients except chicken wings and flour in a large sealable plastic bowl and stir until sugar dissolves. Marinate chicken in sealed container in refrigerator for several hours or overnight, turning once or twice to coat evenly. Before cooking, drain thoroughly, and coat lightly with flour. Fry in vegetable oil until cooked through, (about 10 minutes) on medium high heat being careful not to burn. Drain and serve.

BAGNA CAUDA
"Food of the Gods"

The bagna cauda sits in the middle of the table in a pot (clay or iron) warmed by one candle. It must never boil.

1 C. good olive oil
1/2 C. butter
1/2 oz. anchovy fillets, chopped coarsely
20 cloves garlic, peeled
1/2 C. cream reduced to 1/4 C. (optional)
coarse, crusty bread and vegetables for dipping

In a heavy bottom saucepan, melt butter in olive oil over very low heat. Add anchovies and garlic and cook 1/2 to 1 hour gently, never allowing to boil. The next step is the source of much argument. It calls for whisking in the cream to make a smooth sauce. Some say, absolutely not! No cream! We like it both ways, so...judge for yourself. I like adding a ground dried porcini mushroom. Serve warm with crusty bread and/or vegetables if you like. Our family makes a meal of this with a salad and red wine. Too good for mere mortals??

GARLIC HERB FONDUE

If you haven't used your fondue pot since the 60's here's your chance to get it back into service with this new twist on the traditional Bagna Cauda.

8 cloves fresh garlic, chopped
6 anchovy fillets, rinsed
1 Tbls. each fresh parsley, rosemary,
        oregano and thyme
1/2 tsp. chili flakes
zest of one lemon
1/2 C. sweet butter
1/2 C. good olive oil
fresh ground black pepper
1/2 C. heavy cream

Pureé garlic, anchovies, herbs and zest in a food processor. Heat butter and oil until the butter melts. Stir in the garlic mixture and chili flakes and cook gently for 5 minutes. Add black pepper to taste. (This mixture may be stored for 2-3 days in the refrigerator.) Before serving reheat the mixture in the fondue pot over low heat. Stir in the cream and heat (never boil). Serve with cooked seafood (shrimp, crab, scallops, etc.), vegetables and crusty bread.

Caryl Simpson
Garlic Festival Foods
Gilroy, California

SAVORY GARLIC CHEESECAKE

1/4 C. grated Parmesan cheese
1/4 C. Italian bread crumbs
2 C. heavy cream
2 C. feta cheese, crumbled
3 8-oz. pkgs. cream cheese cut into cubes and softened
5 bulbs baked garlic (see baked garlic recipe, pg. 20)
1/4 C. chives or garlic greens, chopped
1 tsp. each thyme and oregano, chopped
4 large eggs

In a bowl combine the Parmesan and bread crumbs and coat the inside of a well buttered round cake pan, shaking out excess. In a saucepan scald the cream and set aside. Squeeze soft garlic out of their skins into a large bowl. With an electric mixer blend the garlic, feta and 1/4 cup of the cream until mixture is smooth. Add half the cream cheese and 1/2 the remaining cream and beat until smooth. Repeat with remaining cream cheese and cream. Beat in the eggs one at a time until smooth. Stir in the chives and herbs. Pour the batter into the prepared pan. Bake on the lower shelf of a 325° oven for 1 - 1/4 hours or until center is firm. Let cheesecake cool completely on a rack. Unmold onto a platter. Optional: Garnish with marinated sun-dried tomatoes. Serve with wafers, crusty baguettes or bagel chips.

Caryl Simpson
Garlic Festival Foods
Gilroy, California

SAVORY MUSHROOM SPREAD

2 - 3 Tbls. butter or margarine
1/2 lb. fresh mushrooms, chopped
    (Any combination of button or specialty such as
    oyster, shitake or porcini)
1 Tbls. shallots, minced
4 cloves garlic, minced
1 Tbls. dry white wine
2 Tbls. toasted pine nuts or almonds
2 Tbls. sour cream
salt and fresh ground pepper

    Melt the butter in a skillet. Add mushrooms, shallots and garlic and sauté for approximately 6 minutes. Add wine and cook for 1 - 2 minutes longer on medium high heat. Cool mixture. Remove to a serving bowl and stir in sour cream and nuts. Season to taste with salt & pepper.

    Serve with baguettes or crackers

Pikled Garlik Co.
Pacific Grove, California

TORTILLA CHEESE SNACK

1 egg
1/2 tsp. red pepper sauce
1 pkg. large flour tortillas
5 tsp. mild taco sauce
1-1/4 C. shredded Monterey Jack cheese
2/3 C. sliced green onions
1/2 C. chopped Pikled Garlik, (Jalapeno)
1/4 C. vegetable oil

Beat eggs and pepper sauce until smooth. Brush each of 5 tortillas with about 2 tsp. egg mixture and 1 tsp. taco sauce. Sprinkle each of the tortillas with 1/4 cup of the cheese and 2 tsp. of the Pikled Garlik to within 1/2 inch of edge; sprinkle with 2 Tbls. green onions. Top each with 1 tortilla, pressing edges firmly together to seal.

Heat oil in 10 inch skillet over medium heat until hot. Fry 1 tortilla sandwich at a time, turning once, until golden brown, 2-3 minutes; drain. Place on paper towel on cookie sheet; keep warm in 200° oven. Repeat with remaining tortilla sandwiches, adding more oil if necessary. Cut each tortilla sandwich into 8 wedges. Serve.

ROASTED BELL PEPPERS & GARLIC

4 lg. red and/or yellow bell peppers,
      charred and peeled
4 Tbls. virgin olive oil
12 cloves garlic, peeled and thinly sliced
salt
black pepper coarsely ground
Balsamic vinegar

      Cut peppers in 1 inch strips. In a skillet, heat oil over medium beat, add garlic and sauté until golden. Remove from heat, add peppers, sprinkle with salt and pepper and toss. Sprinkle with Balsamic vinegar and serve at room temperature.

Favorite Recipe

Jo Ferrome
Fairfield, Connecticut
Connecticut Garlicfest

ROASTED PEPPERS WITH GARLIC

6 bell peppers
4 cloves garlic, halved
1/4 C. extra virgin olive oil
1 dash red pepper flakes
1 Tbls. tiny capers
1 can California small pitted olives
Optional;
1 can anchovy fillets

Wash peppers and pat dry. Slice in half
lengthwise and clean out pulp. Place on cookie
sheet skin side up. Place under broiler at
highest elevation until skin chars. Remove from
oven and place in a brown paper bag until
cooled somewhat. When cooled, scrape off
burnt skin with a small sharp knife.
(If necessary, rinse off excess burnt skin under
cold water and pat dry.) Slice halves into 1/8
inch strips. Place in casserole dish. Add halved
garlic cloves. Pour olive oil over peppers and
add seasoning. If using anchovies, drain 1/2 of
the oil from can and add to mixture, setting
aside anchovies. Wash and drain capers and
add to mixture; toss. Refrigerate overnight.
When ready to serve, place on platter and
garnish with olives and anchovies. Serve at
room temperature, with Italian bread.

This dish can be prepared and stored in
the refrigerator for up to one week. Cover tightly.

Can be served as an appetizer or as a
side dish with meat, poultry, or fish.

VAMPIRE'S BANE

Soups and Salads

BASIC GARLIC VINAIGRETTE

1/2 C. virgin olive oil
3-4 Tbls. Balsamic Vinegar
2 cloves minced garlic
salt and fresh ground black pepper

Whisk all ingredients together and pour over salad.

GARLIC MUSTARD VINAIGRETTE

3 garlic cloves, finely minced
2 Tbls. Dijon or Garlic Festival® Sweet & Spicy Garlic Mustard
juice of two lemons
1 Tbls. chopped Italian parsley
salt and pepper to taste
1/2 C. olive oil

Whisk all ingredients together and pour over salad.

GARLIC SHERRY VINAIGRETTE

4 Tbls. olive oil
2 Tbls. Sherry
1 Tbls. red wine vinegar or Balsamic Vinegar
2 lg. cloves garlic, minced
2 Tbls. parsley, minced
salt and fresh ground pepper

     Mix all ingredients in non-reactive bowl and store in refrigerator.

CHEESY GARLIC DRESSING

4 Tbls. white wine vinegar
2 lg. cloves garlic, minced
1/2 tsp. crushed red chili flakes
2 Tbls. finely grated Parmesan cheese
1/3 C. good olive oil

     Whisk all ingredients together and pour over salad.

CONFETTI SQUASH SALAD

1 lb. small zucchini
1 lb. small yellow squash
1 red bell pepper, julienned
1/4 C. fresh lemon juice
3 Tbls. minced garlic
2 Tbls. fresh minced basil
1 Tbls. fresh oregano, minced
2 Tbls. virgin olive oil
salt and pepper to taste

     In boiling water simmer squash just until tender. Drain and chill in ice water. Trim ends, cut in half lengthwise, seed, and slice into 3/8 inch slices. Place in bowl with pepper. Combine all other ingredients for dressing and toss with squash.

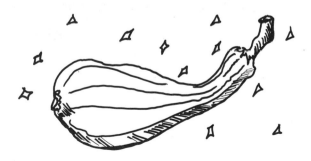

ARTICHOKE WITH ROASTED GARLIC AIOLI

1 large artichoke, per person
1 bulb garlic
1/2 C. mayonnaise
1 tsp. mustard; dijon or sweet & spicy Garlic Festival
        mustard
black pepper

Steam or boil 1 large artichoke per person. Let cool!

Traditional aioli, like mayonnaise, is made with raw eggs. Because of the increased incidence of salmonella we have modified this recipe for safety's sake.

Roast a whole head of garlic (see roasted garlic) and cool. Squeeze the tender garlic cloves to extract the creamy flesh. Mix with the mayonnaise, a grind of black pepper and mustard. Blend until smooth. Serve artichoke on a saucer with aioli for dipping.

May be served as an appetizer or salad.

ITALIAN POTATO SALAD WITH GARLIC & GREEN ONIONS

4 lg. russet potatoes
4 green onions, thinly sliced (white & light green parts)
1/4 C. minced Italian parsley
3 cloves garlic, finely minced
2 Tbls. lemon juice
salt and fresh ground pepper
6 Tbls. extra virgin olive oil

Cook potatoes in boiling water until tender. Cool, peel and slice 1/4 inch thick. Add green onions, parsley and toss gently. In a small skillet briefly sauté garlic in 1/2 olive oil (don't brown), remove from burner, add the rest of the olive oil, lemon juice, salt and fresh ground pepper. Whisk to blend and pour over potatoes. Toss to coat and serve at room temperature.

SPICY PASTA SALAD

1 Tbls. sesame oil
2 Tbls. vegetable oil
1 bunch sliced green onions with some of the greens
8-10 lg. garlic cloves, chopped
1 tsp. chili flakes
1/2 C. apple cider or wine vinegar
1/2 tsp. Chinese 5 spice
1/4 C. soy sauce
1 lb. spaghetti
1 large cucumber, seeded and diced
1 Tbls. toasted sesame seeds

Cook pasta until al denté. Meanwhile, briefly sauté garlic and onion in vegetable oil in a large skillet. Add sesame oil and all other ingredients and heat. Drain pasta and toss in garlic mixture. Remove to bowl and chill. Serve garnished with chopped seeded cucumbers and toasted sesame seeds.

The Colorado Garlic Festival

Denver, Colorado

The Colorado festival is a week long Epicurean adventure exploring the garlicky fare of many of Denver's finest restaurants. The festival also features such activities as a garlic peeling contest, Garlic Lover of the Year (a writing contest), Garlic Tasting and Cook-Off and lectures on garlic and health benefits.

ROASTED GARLIC & BROCCOLI SALAD

3 heads of garlic; peel cloves and place in shallow roasting pan. Mix with 2 Tbls. olive oil and roast at 475° for approximately 20 - 30 minutes, (until just tinged brown).

1 lb. broccoli flowerettes
2 Tbls. soy sauce
1 Tbls. sugar
1 Tsp. sesame oil
1 tsp. roasted sesame seeds

     Cook broccoli briefly 3 - 4 minutes in boiling water. Remove, drain and immerse in ice water. Drain. In a shallow glass bowl mix soy, sugar, and sesame oil until sugar dissolves. Toss with broccoli and cooled garlic until coated. Sprinkle with sesame seeds.

Favorite Recipe

MARINATED SHRIMP & SNOW PEAS

2 lbs. fresh shrimp
1 lb. snow peas, blanched
1/2 C. cilantro leaves
4-5 cloves garlic, minced
juice of two lemons
1/3 C. olive oil
1/4 C. blanched almonds
salt and pepper to taste

       Add shrimp to boiling water and cook about three minutes, just until pink. Rinse with cold water, peel and devein. Toss shrimp and pea pods with the lemon juice. In a food processor pureé cilantro, garlic, oil, almonds, salt and pepper. Toss the pesto with shrimp and peas. Refrigerate until serving. Serve in butter lettuce cups.

ORIENTAL SEAFOOD SALAD

1/2 lb. medium shrimp
1/2 lb. scallops
1 head Romaine, washed and dried
10 wonton skins cut into narrow strips
1/2 C. slivered almonds
vegetable oil for frying

Dressing:

1/4 C. cilantro leaves
3 green onions, whites and light greens sliced thinly
3 cloves garlic, peeled
1 slice fresh ginger, peeled
2-3 Tbls. red wine vinegar
1 Tbls. each; sesame oil and vegetable oil
1 tsp. chili oil (or 1/2 tsp. crushed red chili flakes)
1 tsp. sugar
1/2 tsp. salt

Fry wonton skins in vegetable oil until crispy light brown, drain on paper towels and set aside. Combine all dressing ingredients except green onions in food processor and process until well blended. Add green onions. Prepare shrimp by cooking just until pink (3-4 minutes) in boiling, salted water. Remove with slotted spoon and rinse with cold water. Shell and devein. Cook the scallops until firm (about 5 minutes) in the same water. Remove and rinse. Pat shrimp and scallops dry. Cut both into 1/4 inch slices. Cut romaine into strips and chill. To assemble; place lettuce and seafood in a large chilled bowl and toss with dressing. Add wonton strips and toss again gently. Sprinkle with almonds and serve.

Pikled Garlic Co.
Pacific Grove, California

PIKLED GARLIK SALAD

2 bunches Romaine, torn into bite size pieces
1 large tomato, cored and cut in wedges
1/2 cup Pikled Garlik, chopped
3 Tbls. wine vinegar
1-1/2 Tbls. sugar
1/8 tsp. crushed hot red chilies
1 Tbls. salad oil
1/4 lb. sliced dry salami, cut in 1/4 inch wide strips

      In a large bowl combine Romaine, tomato, and Pikled Garlik; set aside. Stir together wine vinegar, sugar, and crushed hot red chilies. In an 8-to-10 inch frying pan, combine salad oil and dry salami; stir over medium heat until salami is lightly browned. Add vinegar mixture and stir until hot. Pour over greens and mix.

      Makes 4 servings.

ITALIAN SPAGHETTI SOUP WITH GARLIC & TOMATOES

1 C. dry lentils
1 large onion, minced
2 carrots, diced
2 stalks of celery, sliced
6 large garlic cloves, minced
2 C. canned tomatoes in pureé, chopped
4 oz. spaghetti, broken in 2 inch lengths
salt and pepper to taste
2 C. sliced leafy greens; such as spinach, etc.
1/4 C. extra virgin olive oil

Place all ingredients, except spaghetti and greens, in a large kettle with two quarts of water and bring to a boil. Cover and simmer about 1 hour. Adjust seasoning, add spaghetti and greens and simmer an additional 10-12 minutes, until spaghetti is tender. Drain. Add a small drizzle of olive oil to each bowl when serving.

CANYON RANCH GARLIC SOUP

Canyon Ranch is a Spa in Tucson, Arizona, which is dedicated to promoting a healthy lifestyle. Garlic is often featured on their elegant menus and this soup contains only 75 calories per serving.

4 C. chicken broth
10 lg. fresh garlic cloves, peeled
1 lg. tomato, peeled and seeded
1/4 tsp. salt (omit if broth is salted)
1/8 tsp. black pepper
1/4 tsp. dried thyme
2 egg whites
1/2 C. Monterey Jack cheese, grated

Pour 1 cup chicken broth into a large saucepan. Add garlic and bring to a boil. Cover and simmer for 15 minutes. Pour into a blender. Add tomato, salt, pepper and thyme and blend until smooth. Return blended mixture to pan, add remaining broth and bring to a boil. Simmer uncovered for 15 minutes. Beat egg whites with a fork until frothy and gradually add to soup. Mix well and cook for 5 minutes more. Ladle into bowls and sprinkle each with 1 Tbls. grated cheese.

Makes 8 servings

61

The Stinking Rose
San Francisco, California

A Garlic Restaurant

All you have to do is follow your nose and it will lead you to San Francisco's unique and entertaining dining experience; nestled in the heart of North Beach, San Francisco's renowned "Little Italy". A warm, cozy and fun restaurant featuring diverse garlic specialties topped off with their delicious garlic ice cream. We always enjoy it and love taking friends there. Many thanks to owner Dante Serafini for the recipes. Don't miss this one when you're in the City by the Bay.

"WE SEASON OUR GARLIC WITH FOOD!"

The Stinking Rose
San Francisco, California

ZUPPA DI PESCE

32 clams (washed)
24 mussels (washed and bearded)
4 oz. red snapper
4 crab claws
8 medium prawns
4 tsp. chopped garlic
4 tsp. chopped shallots
1 C. white wine
2 C. canned tomato sauce
2 C. fish or vegetable stock
olive oil

     In a large sauté pan, heat a little olive oil. Add shellfish, garlic and shallots. Sauté 1 minute. Add remaining ingredients. Cover and simmer until shellfish open.

     Serves 4

Steve Vekich
Fresh Garlic Association

FRANA GERICA
GARLIC SOUP

2 heads fresh garlic, separated and peeled
2 C. water
1 14-oz. can chicken broth
1 medium onion, diced
2 carrots, diced
3 small potatoes, diced
1 C. chopped celery
1/2 tsp. basil
2 tsp. chopped parsley
slivers of prosciutto (optional) or chopped
       parsley for garnish

      Place garlic cloves and water in saucepan and boil for 5 minutes. Drain off water from pan and add chicken broth, onion, carrots and potatoes. Bring to a boil and add celery, basil and parsley. Simmer for 30 minutes. Let cool slightly, place in blender, and blend until smooth. Return to rinsed pan and reheat, adding a little boiling water if soup is too thick. Taste for seasoning. Ladle into bowls and top with slivers of prosciutto, or additional chopped parsley.

      Makes 4 servings

Dr. Irwin Ziment

DR. IRWIN ZIMENT'S PRESCRIPTION GARLIC SOUP

Garlic is the most widely recognized medicinal herb. It is used across every culture to fight infections and illness of all kinds. It is also reportedly helpful in reducing cholesterol and blood pressure as well as relieving bronchitis. Medical science today is also investigating garlic's role in resisting heart disease, stroke, cancer and many types of infection.

28 oz. chicken broth
1 bulb garlic
5 sprigs parsley, minced
6 sprigs cilantro
1 tsp. each: lemon pepper, minced mint leaves, minced basil leaves, and curry powder

Peel the cloves and place in a pot with the other ingredients. Bring to a boil and simmer for 30 minutes. Inhale the fumes during preparation. Drink the soup, one cup before each meal until finished. (strain first if desired.) Ziment's patients are encouraged to add chili pepper flakes or vegetables to taste.

GARLIC SOUP
OR SOPA DE AJO

2 qts. chicken broth (boil chicken parts: 1 bulb garlic cloves, peeled; 1 Tbls. parsley; 1 lg. chopped carrot; 4 stalks celery; and 4 qts. water for one hour and strain)

1 Tbls. parsley
20 cloves garlic
2 Tbls. soy sauce
1/4 C. sherry
salt and pepper to taste

      Simmer ingredients for 1 hour, strain and season to taste. You may add vegetables if desired.

Favorite Recipe

GARLIC, ONION &
SPINACH SOUP

12 cloves garlic, chopped
2 bunches green onions (whites and light greens),
      chopped
4 med. potatoes, peeled and cubed
1 pkg. frozen chopped spinach, thawed and drained
3 Tbls. butter and margarine
3 Tbls. flour
1 qt. chicken stock
1 pt. cream
salt and pepper

      Sauté the green onions and garlic in butter
briefly; 2-3 minutes. Add the flour and stir, mixing well.
Slowly pour in the chicken stock, stirring constantly.
Bring the mixture to a boil. Add the potatoes and
simmer until tender. Add salt, pepper, spinach and
cream. Simmer briefly uncovered and serve.

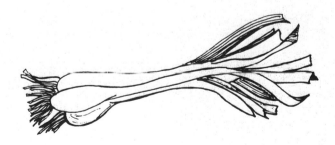

John Heimer
Toledo, Ohio

GAZPACHO

Originally a simple peasant dish made only of bread, garlic, salt, vinegar, oil and water. The discovery of tomatoes in the New World added a new dimension.

1 ea. red and green bell peppers, seeded and
      coarsely chopped
6 large ripe tomatoes (in season) or canned (use the
      juice in place of tomato juice)
1 lg. onion
2 med. cucumbers, peeled and seeded
6-8 cloves garlic
1 C. crumbled French bread, crust removed
2 Tbls. tomato paste (or catsup)
3 C. tomato juice
4 Tbls. olive oil
1/4 C. red wine or Balsamic vinegar
1 Tbls. mild paprika
1/8 tsp. cumin
salt and pepper to taste
bottled hot sauce, to taste
Garnishes: chopped onion, cucumbers, chives,
      croutons, peppers

Pureé the peppers, tomatoes, onion, garlic and bread together in a food processor. Transfer to a large bowl. Mix tomato paste into tomato juice and mix well into pureéd mixture. Whisk in the oil, vinegar, paprika, salt, pepper and cumin. Cover and refrigerate several hours or overnight before serving. Serve cold with garnishes and hot sauce.

Caryl Simpson
Garlic Festival Foods
Gilroy, California

ALI-UUM SOUP

6 slices rye or extra sourdough bread, crusts removed
        and cut into cubes
4 Tbls. butter or margarine
10 lg. garlic cloves, minced finely
1 lg. can (49 oz.) chicken stock
6 eggs
3 tsp. lemon juice
salt and pepper to taste
fresh cilantro, chopped for garnish

       In a skillet melt the butter and add the garlic and bread cubes. Cook over medium heat until cubes are golden and crisp. Remove cubes and set aside. Scrape the skillet remains into a pot and add the stock and lemon juice. Simmer for about 20-30 minutes. Just before serving break eggs, one at a time onto a saucer and slide gently into simmering broth. Poach until set, about 4-5 minutes. Spoon an egg into each of six bowls, ladle broth into bowl and garnish with garlic croutons and cilantro.

GARLIC &
BLACK BEAN SOUP

Black beans are a favorite in Central America and have, along with garlic, become a favorite in the United States. These are also the beans long used by the Chinese, who ferment them for use in recipes and to make black bean sauce.

3 jalapeno chilies, seeded and chopped
2 C. black beans, cleaned and soaked overnight
2 carrots, chopped
1 Tbls. olive oil
1 med. onion, chopped
8 cloves garlic, minced
1 smoked ham hock
1/2 tsp. cumin
8 C. chicken stock
2 Tbls. red wine vinegar
1 8-oz. can tomatoes, chopped and juice
3 Tbls. dry sherry

Sauté the onion, garlic, chilies, and carrots until garlic and onion are soft. Combine this mixture with beans, ham hock, cumin and stock. Bring to a boil, reduce heat and simmer until beans are soft, approx. 1-1/2 hours. Add vinegar and tomatoes and cook additional half hour. Remove ham hock, shred the meat and reserve. Pureé the bean mixture. Return to the saucepan and stir in the sherry and heat. Stir in the shredded ham and serve garnished with cilantro.

Tom Reed
Gilroy, California

GARLIC FESTIVAL
MINESTRONE

This is a wonderful meal, summer or winter.

Garlic paste:

2 Tbls. Garli Garni™
2 Tbls. water
2 Tbls. Garli Ghetti
2 Tbls. olive oil
1/4-1/2 C. fresh basil, chopped
1 Tbls. butter, soft
salt and fresh ground pepper

To prepare paste: In a food processor combine all
paste ingredients and set aside.

Soup:

2 qts. chicken broth
2 C. chopped cabbage
1-1/2 cup small uncooked pasta
1 C. each celery, carrots, green or yellow beans
1 can kidney beans, drained
2 C. sliced zucchini

In a stockpot bring broth to a boil. Add
cabbage, carrots, celery, and green beans and
simmer, covered, until tender. Add kidney beans,
zucchini, pasta, and paste and simmer until pasta is
done (about 6 minutes)

ZUPPA DI AGLIO CARCIOFI E PATATE

25 garlic cloves
3 fresh artichoke hearts
1 lb. white potatoes
3 Tbls. extra virgin olive oil
thyme
Italian parsley
chicken stock (fresh)
salt and pepper

Prior to cooking, prepare the artichokes and potatoes. With the artichoke hearts, soak in water with lemon to prevent darkness. (Note: Do not use the rough center of the artichoke.) Peel and cut the potatoes into small cubes.

In a 2 quart pan, put the extra virgin olive oil and garlic. Sauté until golden in color. Add the potatoes and artichokes and cook for 10 minutes over low heat. Add 1 tsp. salt, 1/2 tsp. pepper and a bunch of thyme. Add one quart of chicken stock. Cook until thickened. Garnish with freshly chopped Italian parsley and one garlic clove. Serve.

THE STINKING ROSE

Side dishes, vegetables, breads, miscellaneous.

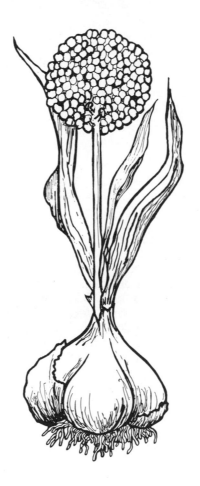

PASTA & POTATOES
WITH PESTO

Pesto:

1-1/2 C. fresh basil
1/2 C. grated Parmesan or Romano cheese
1/4 C. pine nuts (walnuts or almonds)
4-5 cloves fresh garlic
1/3-1/2 C. virgin olive oil

      Place all ingredients (except oil) in food processor and process well. With machine running pour in oil and blend to the consistency of soft butter. Refrigerate or freeze until used. Use on pasta, vegetables, fish, etc. Salt to taste.

Main Dish:

1/4 lb. fresh green beans, sliced into 1/2 inch pieces
1 lg. potato, peeled and chopped coarsely
1/2 lb. pasta
1/2 cup pesto
2 Tbls. butter or margarine

      In a covered saucepan cook beans in salted boiling water for 2-3 minutes. Add potato and cook until tender (8-10 minutes). Meanwhile cook pasta until al denté. Drain pasta and vegetables reserving small amount (2-3 Tbls.) liquid. Mix liquid into pesto and toss with butter, pasta, and vegetables until well coated. Salt and pepper to taste. Serve with Parmesan cheese, if desired.

Arizona's Own Garlic Festival

Verde Valley, Arizona

In June of each year there's a "stinkin" weekend in Verde Valley, Arizona, which hosts not one, but two garlic festivals. An estimated 10,000 people flock to Verde Valley to celebrate the culinary versatility of the "stinking rose". San Dominique Winery's Festival was started by cellarmaster Bill Stalteri and garlic farmer Charles Onion (really!). San Dominique's is small and has "atmosphere" and is held to promote the winery.

Onion decided to launch his own festival nine miles away. This festival features garlicky food such as garlic beef sandwiches and fritters with garlic sauce.

The two day event raises money for many social agencies and civic organizations as well as providing a weekend of family fun and food. Besides indulging in the good food be sure and belly up to the "Garlic Shooter" bar. Yep, you read right! Garlic Shooters!! The most fun, new easy way to have your clove a day.

Update! We have just been informed that the festival will be moved to Sedona, Arizona, in 1994.

FOUL MEAMMAS
(FAVA BEANS)

2 C. dry fava beans
1 tsp. baking soda
1 medium onion, chopped
2 cloves fresh garlic, mashed
2 diced tomatoes
1 lemon, juiced
1 Tbls. olive oil
dash salt and pepper

Soak the fava beans overnight in water with the baking soda. Replace the water the next day with fresh and boil beans one hour until tender. Drain off water. Add remaining ingredients and mix thoroughly until half the beans are broken.

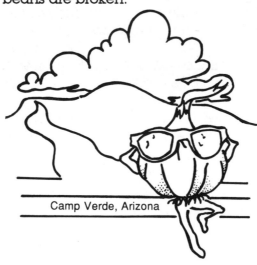

Camp Verde, Arizona

76

FAVA BEANS WITH GARLIC & LEMON

Remove fava beans from their pods and steam them for a few minutes. Remove skins. Sauté in olive oil, lots of garlic, lemon juice and chopped fresh basil. Serve warm or cold.

GARLIC FESTIVAL SALSA

2 anchovy fillets, minced
2 green onions, chopped
4 cloves fresh garlic or 2 tsp. Garli Garni™
2 lg. ripe tomatoes, chopped
1 cucumber, seeded and diced
1/2 C. pitted black olives, diced
2 Tbls. olive oil
2 tsp. capers
dash hot pepper sauce, to taste
2 Tbls. lime juice

Mix all ingredients in bowl and refrigerate at least 1 hour. Serve with chips, tacos, or accompanying meat.

Janice Hopkins
Miami, Florida

TABOULI

In the Middle East, wheat is used as often as Far Easterners use rice, and in everything from soups to salads. Tabouli is a traditional dish made with bulgur wheat that has been parboiled, dried and cracked. It is nutritious and a great substitute for potatoes, rice or noodles.

1 C. bulgur
1/2 C. warm water
1 lg. ripe tomato, peeled and chopped
1/2 C. chopped parsley
2 Tbls. finely chopped green onions
1 Tbls. chopped fresh mint
1/2 tsp. salt, pepper to taste
1/4 C. lemon juice
minced garlic to taste (we like lots!)
2 Tbls. cooking oil
1 Tbls. olive oil
lettuce
plain yogurt

In a bowl combine bulgur and warm water. Let stand one hour. Stir in tomato, parsley, onion, mint, salt and pepper. In a small skillet in cooking oil briefly sauté garlic and cool. Combine with lemon juice and olive oil and toss with bulgur. Cover and chill. Serve on bed of lettuce with yogurt.

Serves 6.

Heather Simpson
Gilroy, California

FRIED GARLICKY BREAD BALLS

1 tsp. salt
2 C. flour
3 tsp. baking powder
3 tsp. curry powder
2 small hot chilies, seeded and minced
1 small onion, minced
6 fresh garlic cloves, minced
1 tsp. minced ginger
1 C. watercress, minced
1-1/2 C. water
1 qt. vegetable oil

Combine all ingredients except oil in a bowl. Let stand for one hour. Heat the oil in heavy skillet, drop the dough by spoonfuls into the oil and fry until brown. Drain on paper towel and serve hot.

James Sedgwick
Castroville, California

ARTICHOKES WITH GARLIC BUTTER SAUCE

Castroville, California is the Artichoke Capital of the World and just down the road from the "Garlic Capital of the World". Garlic and artichokes are a perfect pairing.

4 medium artichokes
1 C. dry white wine
8 cloves garlic, minced finely
1 Tbls. lemon juice, fresh
1/2 tsp. oregano and basil
3 Tbls. butter, chilled
minced parsley for garnish

Trim stems of artichokes so they stand upright in a deep pot with 3 inches of boiling water. Cover and steam 30-40 minutes until tender. Drain. In a small saucepan simmer the wine and garlic until reduced by 1/2. Add lemon juice and herbs and reduce heat. Slowly add butter stirring constantly until sauce thickens. Garnish and serve with artichokes.

Bradley Ogden
Compton Place Restaurant
San Francisco, California

BRADLEY OGDEN'S GARLIC MASHED POTATOES

Chef Bradley Ogden was formerly Executive Chef at the acclaimed Compton Place Restaurant in San Francisco where his innovative interpretations of American classics earned him well deserved acclaim. Now proprietor of his own restaurant, the Lark Creek Inn in Marin County, Ogden draws upon a rich American culinary heritage to create a menu that is purely American, albeit with some great touches such as the garlic cloves added to this superb version of potato pureé.

2 lbs. small red potatoes, peeled
1 lg. head fresh garlic
1-1/2 C. heavy cream
1-1/2 C. milk
6 Tbls. butter
salt and white pepper

Cook potatoes in salted boiling water until tender (about 20 minutes). Drain and dry in 350° oven for 10 minutes. Meanwhile separate and peel garlic cloves. Simmer cloves with cream, milk and butter for 30 minutes until garlic is soft. Using a blender, pureé potatoes and garlic cream mixture. Season to taste with salt and pepper. Thin with more cream if necessary.

GARLIC PULL-APART BREAD

This is great for a party or brunch and smells heavenly.

2 loaves frozen white or wheat (or both)
        bread dough, thawed
1/2 C. butter or margarine
1/4 C. dried basil and oregano
1/2 C. onion, chopped fine
6-8 cloves garlic, minced

Cut off pieces of dough the size of golf balls. Place in a layer in a greased bundt pan. Meanwhile briefly (1-2 minutes) sauté garlic and onion in butter or margarine, cool slightly and add herbs. Spoon some of the butter mixture over first layer and repeat until all the bread balls are used. Cover and allow to rise until doubled in size. Bake at 375° for 30-35 minutes until golden. Cool and unmold. (If you would like cheesy garlic pull-apart, add cheese between the layers.)

Caryl Simpson
President- Garlic Festival Foods
Gilroy, California

COUNTRY VEGETABLE & GARLIC RAGOUT

This is a great way to use the bounty of your garden or of the Farmers Market and can change with the season. Squash, peppers, eggplant, beans, onion; any combination will be delicious. Sauté each vegetable separately until al denté. Season each with salt and pepper and set aside. In the same pan cook thinly sliced onion and lots of garlic briefly. Add a little white wine and some chopped ripe tomatoes and cook on high heat to evaporate liquid. Toss with the cooked vegetables, fresh herbs and a drizzle of good olive oil. Let stand for a half hour or so to meld the flavors. Serve with thick slices of toasted bread or as a meat or bean accompaniment.

GREENS 'N GARLIC

1/3 C. chicken or vegetable stock
8-10 cloves garlic, roasted (see roasted garlic recipe)
1 bunch chard or spinach, stemmed
2 Tbls. ea. lemon juice and tomato juice
1 Tbls. good olive oil
1/2 tsp. pepper flakes
toasted coarse bread (peasant or sourdough)

      Steam chard until tender. In a large bowl whisk lemon juice, tomato juice, oil and pepper. Toss with chard to coat. To serve, spread bread with roasted garlic, mound on bread.

GARLICKY LEMON
GRILLING SAUCE

1 stick butter or margarine
juice of 1/2 lemon
1 Tbls. PICKAPEPPA Sauce
1 tsp. hot pepper sauce
5 cloves garlic, finely minced
1/4 tsp. salt
fresh ground black pepper, to taste

      In a medium non-reactive sauce pan melt butter and add all other ingredients, except salt and pepper. Simmer gently for 10 minutes. Season with salt and pepper. Use for fish, poultry, and vegetables.

Favorite Recipe

85

SWEET PICKLED GARLIC

If you have an excess of garlic in your garden, here is a way to prepare and keep it for use in salads, dressing, and just to eat like any other pickle.

8 C. whole peeled garlic cloves
1 C. sugar
1/2 tsp. horseradish
1 tsp. chili flakes
1/2 C. salt
2 Tbls. mustard seed
1 qt. white vinegar
bay leaves

Sprinkle the garlic with salt (in non-reactive bowl), add water to cover and let stand overnight in a cool place. Rinse and drain thoroughly. Simmer all other ingredients gently for 10-15 minutes until sugar is dissolved. Pack garlic into sterilized 8 oz. canning jars leaving 1/2 inch head space. Place one bay leaf in each jar. Pour liquid over garlic. Remove air bubbles and seal. Process for 10 minutes in boiling water.

GARLIC JELLY

1/2 C. fresh garlic, finely chopped
2 C. white wine vinegar
5-1/2 C. sugar
3 C. water
1 package (2 oz.) powdered pectin
1/4 tsp. butter or oil
2 drops food coloring (optional)

Combine garlic and vinegar in a 2 qt. kettle. Simmer mixture gently, uncovered, over medium heat for 15 minutes. Remove pan from heat and pour mixture into a 1 qt. glass jar. Cover and let stand at room temperature for 24 to 36 hours.

Pour flavored vinegar through a wire strainer into a bowl, pressing the garlic with the back of a spoon to squeeze out liquid. Discard any residue. Measure sugar into a dry bowl. Combine the garlic-vinegar solution and the water in a 5 or 6 qt. kettle. Add pectin, stirring well.

Over high heat, bring mixture to a boil, stirring constantly to avoid scorching. Add sugar, and stir well. Bring mixture to a full rolling boil. Add butter to reduce foaming. Continue stirring. Boil the mixture hard for exactly 2 minutes. Remove pan from heat and skim off any foam. Add red, yellow, or orange food coloring if desired. Pour jelly into prepared glasses. Seal according to directions on recipe folder in pectin package.

Makes approximately 5 cups.

GARLIC BASIL SALSA

10-12 Italian Roma tomatoes, chopped
4-6 cloves fresh garlic, minced
1/2-3/4 C. fresh minced basil leaves
1/4 C. minced fresh parsley
1/4 C. good virgin olive oil
juice of 1 lemon or lime
salt and fresh ground pepper, to taste

Combine all ingredients in a food processor with metal blade with several quick pulses. Texture should be chunky. Use on fish, potatoes, crusty bread or vegetables. Spoon on top of a block of cream cheese for an appetizer spread.

Favorite Recipe

QUICK GARLIC FESTIVAL PINEAPPLE SALSA

2 jars Garlic Festival® Salsa
1 small can crushed pineapple in juice
2 Tbls. dark brown sugar

Drain juice from pineapple into a small sauce pan and bring to a simmer. Stir in brown sugar until dissolved. Add pineapple and heat through. Remove from heat and stir in Garlic Festival® Salsa. Allow to cool before serving with meat, fish, or chips.

GARLICKY GREEN SAUCE

2 Tbls. finely chopped onion
6 cloves garlic, minced
1 Tbls. butter or margarine
1 C. soft bread crumbs
1/2 C. parsley leaves
4 Tbls. red wine or Balsamic vinegar
2 Tbls. capers
2 anchovy fillets
1/3 C. virgin olive oil

      In a skillet cook onion and garlic in the butter until onion is soft. Transfer mixture to a blender or food processor. Add all ingredients except oil. Process until smooth. With the machine running, slowly add the olive oil. Serve with meat, fish, poultry, or pasta.

Ken and Jill Heidrick
Moss Beach, California

KEN & JILL'S
GARLIC GRAPES

O.K. folks, admittedly this sounds like a weird one. But..... we garlic lovers are adventurous, right?

cream cheese
enough mayonnaise to thin
minced garlic, to taste
Thompson seedless grapes

Mix and let stand overnight. Stir over grapes.... eat! They swear they're grape, er, great! You be the judge.

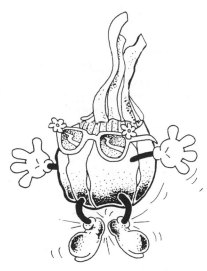

SZECHWAN BRIOCHE

1/3 C. sugar
2 Tbls. yeast
3 eggs, beaten
1 Tbls. fresh ginger, minced
2 Tbls. garlic, minced
3 Tbls. toasted sesame oil
1/2 C. green onion, finely chopped

1 C. milk
3/4 tsp. salt
2 tsp. red pepper flakes
5 C. all purpose flour
1 cube butter, softened
3/4 C. peanuts

Combine sugar, salt and milk in a saucepan. Place over low heat; stir to dissolve sugar and salt. Remove from heat and transfer to a bowl. Let cool to 90°. Stir in dry yeast until dissolved.

In a separate bowl, mix eggs, minced fresh ginger root, minced garlic, toasted sesame oil and red pepper flakes. Add egg mixture and well-softened butter to the milk mixture. Add chopped peanuts and finely chopped green onions. Beating continuously, slowly add the all purpose flour.

Either using a dough hook or beating vigorously, knead about 10 minutes until dough is developed. It will be smooth and elastic with a shiny skin. Add more flour if needed. Place dough in a greased bowl, turn dough to coat and cover with plastic wrap. Let rise in a warm place for 1-1/2 hours, until it doubles. Punch dough and divide in half. Cover and chill until it can be shaped comfortably. The amount of butter in this dough can make it slippery to handle if the weather is warm or it has been in a bit too much heat.

To make garlic bulbs, divide the dough in half. Divide each half into 5 equal parts. Roll each part into a 12 inch "log", tapered at one end and rounded on the other like an elongated pear. Lay 5 of these next to each other on a cooking parchment lined baking sheet and pinch the large part of the pears together to form the bottom of one bulb. Two thirds of the way up, pinch the 5 pears together to form the neck of the bulb. Repeat with the other half of the dough. Proof and bake. Brush gently with an egg wash of 1 egg beaten with 1 tsp. water (be careful not to drip wash inside pan). Bake at 350° for 35-45 minutes. When bread begins to brown, remove it from the oven. Quickly brush on egg wash again and then return it to the oven for 5 minutes. When the brioche is done, a tap produces a hollow sound. The bulbs will have flat backs and have the garlic shape in front.

Just before serving, cut about 6 long green onion tops and fit into the top of each bulb, using a paring knife to poke them in. Let your guests pull the bread apart with their best tools, their hands.

Note: You can freeze the punched, unshaped dough, wrapped if foil, rather than chill it. Then unwrap but cover it and thaw it slowly in the cooler; allow for long proofing.

GREEN GARLIC PESTO

       Here's an idea on how to utilize that garlic that you've kept too long. If it's starting to grow, plant it! Instead of using the bulbs, use the greens. This idea is from Francis Pollack of Rolling Hills Farm in Saylorsburg, Pennsylvania. Use it on pizza or pasta.

1-1/2 C. garlic greens (tops)
1/2 C. olive oil
salt and white pepper, to taste
1/4 C. grated Parmesan cheese

       In a food processor, process all ingredients until smooth. Use on pasta or good coarse bread.

Favorite Recipe

ROASTED GARLI GARNI™ POTATOES

4-5 large scrubbed potatoes with skins
1/2 cube butter or margarine (or olive oil)
1-2 tsp. Garli Garni™ or Lo Salt Garli Garni™
10-12 sprigs fresh rosemary

　　　　Slice clean dry potatoes into large thick fries.
Melt butter or margarine in a heavy oven proof skillet
and sprinkle in Garli Garni™ and rosemary. Place fries
in skillet and toss until coated. Place in 400° oven and
roast for 15 minutes; then toss, scraping the bottom.
Return to oven and roast another 15 minutes or until
done. (Can be eaten as an appetizer.)

Favorite Recipe

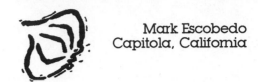

Mark Escobedo
Capitola, California

MARK'S GOURMET MEAL

Mark, our shipping manager is a bachelor. He swears our garlic mustard is all it takes to make a gourmet meal... Take two (or three) slices of white bread, slather on plenty of Garlic Festival Mustard, add 3 slices of folded bologna, 2 slices of American cheese and pickles (optional). Serve with chips and a malted beverage of your choice.

When you call to place an order for more copies of this cookbook, ask to speak to Mark if you'd like some more of his gourmet recipes.

Favorite Recipe

Fresh Garlic Association
Sausalito, California

SAVORY GARLIC BREAD PUDDING

This recipe from the Fresh Garlic Association may be the most delicious bread pudding you've ever served.

1 head garlic, separated into cloves
2 C. bread cubes
2 C. milk
2 Tbls. butter
1 tsp. dried dillweed or 1 Tbls. chopped fresh dill
3 eggs
1 C. heavy cream
garnish: sour cream, paprika, chopped chives and/or
      crumbled cooked bacon

Preheat oven to 325°. Cover garlic cloves with boiling water and let stand for 5 minutes. Drain, peel, and mince finely. Place bread cubes in a buttered 2 qt. rectangular baking dish. Scald milk (heat until bubbles form at edges), and add butter, garlic and dill. Blend 1 cup of the milk with the eggs and cream. Add remaining milk, and pour over bread cubes. Bake for 30 minutes, or until set. Garnish each serving with a dollop of sour cream and sprinkle with paprika, chopped chives, and crumbled bacon. Serve warm, as a brunch dish.

Makes 6 to 8 servings.

POLENTA WITH PORCINI & GARLIC

1 lb. fresh porcini mushrooms or 8 oz. dried
6 cloves fresh garlic, chopped
1 bunch parsley leaves, chopped
1/2 tsp. red pepper flakes
3 Tbls. olive oil
salt and pepper, to taste
Polenta for 6

Clean, trim and chop coarsely the fresh porcini mushrooms. If using dried, soak in very hot water for 15-20 minutes. Drain and pat dry before chopping. In a large skillet over medium heat, brown mushrooms with garlic, parsley, and pepper flakes in olive oil for about 15 minutes. Season with salt and pepper. Prepare polenta (Italian cornmeal) according to instructions (for six). Allow to cool and form patties. Fry in small amount of olive oil until light brown on each side. Top with porcini garlic mixture and serve.

THE BIG BULB

Main dishes, meats, poultry,
seafood & pasta

The Stinking Rose
San Francisco, California

MARINATED CRAB

2 live crabs
6 C. olive oil
1 C. chopped garlic
1/2 C. chopped parsley
2 Tbls. crushed red chili flakes
1/4 C. salt
1/4 C. pepper

     In a large pot, bring water to a boil. Drop crabs in for 1 minute. Remove and clean; then break in half. Combine remaining ingredients and mix well. Put crab in marinade and leave for 4-6 hours. Remove from marinade and place in a roasting pan. Cook at 500° for 10-15 minutes.

PASTA & POTATO WITH GREENS AND GARLIC

Pasta (your choice)
1-2 large potatoes, cubed
Several Tbls. fresh garlic, minced
1 C. fresh basil, cut in strips
1/2-3/4 C. good olive oil
salt and pepper, to taste
fresh grated Romano cheese

Cook pasta and potatoes together. Drain. Combine other ingredients, except cheese, in a large bowl. Add the drained pasta and potatoes and toss. Sprinkle with cheese.

Favorite Recipe

SPAGHETTI WITH GARLIC & OLIVE OIL

This classic couldn't be easier; or better.

as much minced garlic as you dare
extra virgin olive oil
fresh chopped parsley (optional)
crushed red chili flakes, to taste
salt and fresh ground pepper, to taste
pasta

Gently sauté the garlic in olive oil. Stir in the parsley, chili pepper and salt. Cook pasta, drain and toss with garlic and olive oil. Add fresh chopped tomatoes in season. Garnish with grated cheese.

GARLICFEST

Fairfield, Connecticut

"Where garlic reigns and not a tastebud goes home disappointed"

Are you hungering for a truly mouth watering experience? Suffering from the winter doldrums? Have you ever wished you could get to the Garlic Festival in Gilroy, California? Well, Father Bill Sangiovanni and Dr. John Santilli have come up with the answer to your prayers and theirs. In April, Notre Dame High School holds a Garlicfest in Connecticut. It is an overwhelming success and an extravaganza of garlic - laden goodies such as chicken in creamy garlic sauce, vegetables sautéed in garlic with beans, garlic foccaccia bread, stuffed eggplant and garlic prawn rolls. As one newspaper put it, "they came in droves to sample the cloves". With an unexpected attendance of 20,000 garlic lovers, Father Bill and Dr. John have a wild success on their hands.

Patricia Land
Connecticut Garlicfest

AUNT MARY'S NEOPOLITAN CHICKEN

1 lb. chicken breasts, filleted and pounded
1/2 C. flour
2 Tbls. butter (optional)
1/4 C. olive oil
4 - 6 cloves garlic
2 C. chicken stock (or 2 bouillon cubes in 2 C. water)
1 Tbls. lemon juice
1 lemon, sliced
1 Tbls. parsley, coarsely chopped

After washing and pounding chicken breasts, cut into cubes and dredge in flour. Heat oil (and butter if desired) over medium heat. Stir fry chicken until lightly browned and set aside. Mince garlic and sauté in skillet in remaining pan juices; add chicken broth and bring to boil, scraping sides and bottom of skillet. Add lemon juice. Place cooked chicken in casserole dish and cover with broth mixture. Let sit on low heat for at least 1/2 hour to absorb flavors. Serve over rice pilaf. Garnish with sliced lemon and parsley.

This dish may be prepared in advance and refrigerated for 1 - 2 days. Usually taste improves. Just reheat and serve over fresh rice.

Serves 4 - 6

STEAK ALLA MARISA

Steak (1 per person)
cherry peppers (1 per person)
4 oz. fresh mushrooms
3 - 4 pitted black olives
1 Tbls. olive oil
4 cloves garlic, chopped

Grill steak to preference: set aside. Heat oil slightly in skillet. Sauté garlic, cherry peppers, mushrooms and black olives in oil. Top steaks with mixture.

SHRIMP DELLA CASA

1 - 2 lbs. fresh spinach
1 1/2 lbs. shrimp, cleaned and deveined
1 1/2 lbs. fresh pasta
5 - 6 cloves garlic, minced
enough olive oil to cover pan
1/4 C. water
salt and pepper to taste
Optional: hot pepper flakes

Blanch spinach, drain and set aside. Sauté shrimp, garlic, and oil briefly, then add spinach and cook with 1/4 C. water. Add salt, pepper and hot pepper flakes if desired. Pour over pasta and toss.

Serves 4

PASTA WITH ROASTED GARLIC, TOMATOES & BASIL

pasta (your choice) for 4, cheese filled ravioli are great
1/2 C. olive oil
40-50 whole peeled garlic cloves
1/2 C. fresh basil, sliced into thin strips
4 fresh tomatoes, diced
salt and pepper, to taste (for a double dose of garlic,
        substitute Garli Garni™)
fresh grated Parmesan cheese

      Place whole cloves of garlic in a shallow roasting pan with the olive oil. Roast at 350° for approximately 40 minutes, tossing once or twice. They will attain a tan color, soft texture, and a mellow nutty flavor. Meanwhile, cook pasta al denté and drain.

      To serve: Toss with olive oil and garlic, tomatoes and basil. Salt and pepper to taste. Garnish with Parmesan.

PRAWNS WITH GARLIC & SHERRY SAUCE

8 - 10 fresh prawns
1/4 C. extra virgin olive oil
1 Tbls. butter
4 - 5 cloves fresh garlic, chopped
1/3 C. dry Sherry
chopped parsley for garnish

Peel and devein prawns. Cook briefly in olive oil over medium heat just until pink. Remove with slotted spoon. Add garlic and butter to oil and cook 1-2 minutes over medium - high heat, stirring constantly. Remove from heat, cool slightly, then slowly stir in Sherry. Return to heat just until mixture begins to bubble. Pour over shrimp and garnish with parsley.

GARLIC, ONION & PEPPER CONFIT STEAK PIZZA

This is a variation on that perennial Gilroy Garlic Festival favorite, the Pepper Steak Sandwich. A main dish pizza for the meat lovers out there; it only needs a hearty red wine and green salad to make a meal.

2 large Spanish onions, thinly sliced
10 cloves fresh garlic, minced
1 each; red, yellow and green bell peppers, julienned
3-4 Tbls. olive oil
1/2 C. white wine
2 Tbls. each rosemary and oregano

pizza dough or large Boboli shell
1 lb. grilled, rare, flank steak
2 Tbls. pine nuts (optional)
salt and pepper to taste

To make confit: Sauté the onion, garlic and peppers in the olive oil for 3-4 minutes. Add the wine and half the herbs, salt and pepper to taste. Cover and simmer for approx. 10 minutes. Uncover and simmer an additional 5 minutes or until liquid has evaporated. Set aside. On a large cookie sheet or pizza pan place large pizza shell (or 4 small ones) or Boboli. Brush with olive oil and spread with a thick layer of confit. Cook pizza for approx. 20 minutes (or Boboli instructions). Add the steak, sliced into thin strips, and pine nuts (optional) and cook 3-5 minutes longer. Garnish with remaining herbs and fresh ground black pepper and serve.

Garlic World
Gilroy, California

GARLIC WORLD'S PESTO LASAGNA

Lasagna:

1 pkg. lasagna noodles, cooked
12 oz. Mozzarella cheese
4 oz. pesto sauce; homemade (see recipe, pg. 118)
     or prepared
1 C. Ricotta cheese
White sauce (below)
1/2 C. fresh Parmesan cheese, grated

     Mix pesto with Ricotta and white sauce. Spray 9x12 baking dish with a non-stick coating. Layer pasta, Mozzarella, and sauce. Repeat layering, ending with sauce. Sprinkle Parmesan on top. Bake at 325° for 20-25 minutes.

White Sauce:

1 cube butter or margarine
1/2 C. flour
2 C. Half and Half
1/2 tsp. each; salt and fresh ground pepper
dash nutmeg

     Melt butter, add flour and stir until combined. Add cream, whisking constantly until smooth and maintaining smooth consistency. Season with salt and pepper and nutmeg.

CHINESE PIZZA WITH PLUM SAUCE & ROASTED GARLIC

Here is a delicious and different "pizza" with a touch of China and more than a touch of garlic. Individual pizzas make great appetizers.

frozen pizza dough or Boboli
40 cloves roasted garlic (until light brown),
     each cut in half
Plum sauce (available in Chinese section or
     Chinese grocery)
1/2 C. chopped green onions
chopped meat from Chinese duck or cooked
     teriyaki chicken breasts
thin slices of red bell pepper

Preheat oven to 400° or follow Boboli instructions. Oil large cookie sheet or pizza pan. Pat dough into large circle or several small ones. Brush with plum sauce and arrange the garlic, duck or chicken meat, green onions and thin pepper slices evenly over the top. Bake until crust is crisp, about 20 minutes or according to Boboli instructions.

Note: Boboli is an Italian pizza shaped bread shell that can be used to create an infinite variety of homemade "gourmet" pizzas. They are available individually packaged and ready to use in many supermarkets.

GRILLED PIZZAS WITH GARLIC & DRIED TOMATOES

1 lb. loaf white or whole wheat bread dough, thawed
sun-dried tomatoes packed in olive oil (or dried
       tomatoes that have been rehydrated
       in hot water)
olive oil
pesto sauce, homemade, (see recipe pg. 118),
       or prepared
lots of chopped fresh or pickled garlic
1-1/2 -2 C. smoked Mozzarella cheese, shredded

      About 45 minutes before cooking prepare enough briquettes to spread into a single layer in a barbecue with a lid. Light and burn coals until coals are covered with gray ash before spreading into a single layer. Maintain heat at medium level so bread won't burn

      On a floured board divide the dough into four pieces and shape into balls. Roll each into a 6 inch round. Brush with olive oil and place oil side down on a square of aluminum foil. Brush top with oil. Flatten rounds, with your hands, to about 1/8 inch thick. Let stand about 20 minutes until slightly puffy. When coals are ready, flip each from its foil onto the grill and cook until golden brown on the bottom. Remove to a cookie sheet with a spatula, brown side up. Spread with pesto, tomatoes, (which have been drained and chopped-if packed in oil, oil may be used to brush pizzas), garlic, and cheese. Return to the grill. Cover the barbecue with the lid, open vents, and cook until bottom is golden and cheese is melted. Remove from heat. Sprinkle with salt (to taste) and fresh ground pepper.

The Gilroy
Garlic Festival

Gilroy, California

The biggest garlic festival of all! Each year,
approximately 150,000 visitors descend on Gilroy
for three days of garlic mania. The festival is held
in July on the last full 3 day weekend. The
following recipes are compliments of the Fresh
Garlic Association, which formerly published a
newsletter. They are winners of the annual Great
Garlic Cook-Off.

Maria Sandoval
Alameda, California
1991 Gilroy Garlic Festival-First Place Winner

GARLIC & CHILI RELLENO SOUFFLÉ

softened butter and dry bread crumbs for mold
5 Tbls. butter, softened
3 Tbls. all-purpose flour
1 C. hot milk
1/4 tsp. plus 1 pinch salt
1/8 tsp. white pepper
4 large egg yolks, well beaten
1 - 7 oz. can peeled green chilies, drained and patted
        dry, cut in 1 inch pieces
8 cloves fresh garlic, minced
5 large egg whites
1/2 C. grated Monterey Jack cheese

Preheat oven to 375°. Grease a 1-1/2 qt. soufflé mold or Pyrex baking dish generously with butter, and dust well with bread crumbs. Set aside. Heat 3 Tbls. of the butter until it foams, add flour, and cook over medium heat until it starts to brown, stirring constantly. Add hot milk and cook for 4 minutes, stirring constantly, until thickened. Season with 1/4 tsp. of the salt, and white pepper. Let cool slightly and add the beaten egg yolks, then the chilies, and mix well.

Sauté garlic in remaining 2 Tbls. butter until golden brown. Add to the above mixture. Beat egg whites with a pinch of salt until stiff. Fold beaten egg whites into first mixture; then fold in the grated cheese. Pour into prepared mold and bake for 35-40 minutes, until puffed and brown.

Makes 4 to 6 servings.

Rosie Burtchby
Ventura, California
1991 Gilroy Garlic Festival-Third Place Winner

ROSIE'S TERRIBLY SPICY RIBS

1 rack (approx. 4 lbs.) lean pork, cut into double
    rib sections

Marinade:
3 cloves fresh garlic, crushed
1 tsp. minced fresh ginger root
1/2 C. soy sauce
1/2 C. honey
1/2 C. dry sherry
1/2 C. dry vermouth

Coating:
5 Tbls. minced fresh garlic
3 Tbls. minced fresh ginger root
2 Tbls. Oriental sesame oil
1 C. sesame seeds, divided
1 C. finely chopped fresh cilantro, divided

      In glass or stainless steel bowl, combine
marinade ingredients. Add ribs and turn to coat.
Cover with plastic wrap and marinate in refrigerator for
24 hours or longer, turning occasionally. Preheat oven
to 325°. Remove ribs from marinade and pat semi-dry.
Combine coating mixture of garlic, ginger and sesame
oil, and roll ribs in this mixture. Bake for 20 minutes.
Turn ribs, sprinkle with half the sesame seeds and
cilantro, and bake for a further 20 minutes. Turn ribs,
sprinkle with remaining sesame seeds and cilantro,
and bake for 15 minutes more or until tender.

Gilroy Garlic Festival
Kelly Greene
Mill Valley, California

KELLY'S ASIAN CHICKEN

This absolutely mouth-watering chicken dish was unanimously selected as the First Place Winner in the Garlic Recipe Contest and Cook-off in 1978. It's a simple, inspired combination that takes only 20 minutes to put together. Serve with cooked Chinese noodles and then stand back and let the compliments fly!

3-1/2 lbs. frying chicken, cut into serving pieces, or the equivalent in chicken parts of your choice.
3 Tbls. peanut oil
1 bulb (not clove) fresh garlic, peeled and coarsely chopped
2 small dried hot red peppers (optional)
3/4 C. distilled white vinegar
1/4 C. soy sauce
3 Tbls. honey

Heat oil in large, heavy skillet and brown chicken well on all sides, adding garlic and peppers toward the end. Add remaining ingredients and cook over medium high heat until chicken is done and sauce has been reduced somewhat. This will not take long, less than 10 minutes. If you are cooking both white and dark meat, remove white meat first, so it does not dry out. Watch very carefully so that the sauce does not burn or boil away. There should be a quantity of sauce left to serve with the chicken, and the chicken should appear slightly glazed. Serve with Chinese noodles, pasta or rice.

Priscilla Yee
Concord, California

CARAMELIZED GARLIC PHYLLO FOCACCIA

This recipe is the 1992 winning entry in the Great Gilroy Cook-Off. It met all the criteria and delighted the panel of judges who ate up every crumb. Priscilla Yee of Concord, California, teamed up simple ingredients in an imaginative way to create a dish that looked appetizing, made excellent use of garlic, and tasted wonderful. Furthermore, it's easy to make!

12 large cloves fresh garlic, unpeeled
6 1-inch sprigs fresh thyme
3 Tbls. olive oil
1 Tbls. minced fresh garlic
6 sheets phyllo, thawed
1/2 C. grated Parmesan cheese
1 C. shredded mozzarella cheese
1/4 tsp. red pepper flakes
24 fresh basil leaves
4 Roma tomatoes, thinly sliced and seeds removed

Preheat oven to 400°. Place garlic cloves in a greased 1-quart baking dish. Sprinkle thyme on top. Cover dish tightly with foil. Bake for 30 minutes, or until garlic is soft, and reserve. Meanwhile, in a small bowl combine oil and minced garlic. Place 1 sheet phyllo on flat surface. Brush lightly with garlic oil and sprinkle 1 Tbls. Parmesan. Repeat with remaining phyllo sheets, oil, and Parmesan.

Place stack of phyllo, centered, in an ungreased 12-inch round pizza pan. Fold in excess dough at corners towards center, pleating as necessary to fit shape of pan. Layer mozzarella, red pepper flakes, basil leaves, and tomato slices over phyllo, and arrange roasted garlic on surface. Sprinkle with remaining Parmesan. Bake on bottom rack of oven for 15-20 minutes or until golden brown. Cool slightly before serving. Garlic should be squeezed onto focaccia and peels discarded as you eat.

Makes one 12-inch pizza.

116

Caryl Simpson

SAVORY POLENTA "CAKE"

Like pasta, rice and potatoes, polenta is a great canvas for the intense flavors of cheeses, herbs, and condiments such as dried tomatoes. Polenta, coarse ground cornmeal, is a traditional staple of Italian cuisine and with the increased popularity of Italian fare in America, has become popular here as well.

2 C. polenta
1 tsp. each: thyme, oregano, sage (minced or 1/2 tsp.
        each dried)
salt and fresh ground pepper (to taste) or 1 Tbls.
        Garli Garni™
1 each: medium red pepper, green pepper,
        red onion, diced
2 Tbls. butter and 1 Tbls. olive oil
10 cloves fresh garlic, minced
1 lb. cheese, grated (Monterey Jack, cheddar, fontina,
        gorgonzola, or combo.)
spicy tomato sauce, bottled or your own

Sauté onions, peppers and garlic in butter and oil. Set aside. Prepare polenta according to instructions, stirring in herbs. Pour into two round cake pans that have been sprayed with non-stick spray. Refrigerate at least 3 hours or overnight. To serve; invert one layer onto oven proof platter. Sprinkle with 1/2 the cheese, and the onion and pepper mixture. Position second layer on top of first. Sprinkle with rest of cheese and heat in 350° oven just long enough to heat through and melt cheese. Serve with spicy tomato (or marinara) sauce or a mushroom sauce.

117

Tom Reed
Garlic Festival Foods
Gilroy, California

BASIL PESTO

No garlic cookbook would be complete without a good recipe for classic Basil Pesto. This aromatic garlic and basil sauce can become a staple; add it to soups, sauces, pizzas, stews, stuffed mushrooms, or add to pasta salads. Fresh pesto can be frozen in ice cube trays to preserve the taste of summer all through the winter.

2 C. fresh basil
4-5 firm garlic cloves
1/2 C. fresh grated Parmesan cheese
2-3 Tbls. fresh Romano cheese, grated
1/4 C. pine nuts or walnuts
1/2 C. virgin olive oil
salt and fresh ground pepper, to taste

Combine all ingredients except oil in a food processor. With machine running, slowly add oil. Let stand several minutes before serving.

SCAMPI

1 stick sweet butter
1-2 Tbls. Garli Garni™ or fresh minced garlic
2 Lbs. large cleaned shrimp or prawns
lemon slices
3 Tbls. olive oil
1/4 C. dry white wine

      Melt butter in a large skillet on medium heat, add oil, Garli Garni® and wine. Add prawns and sauté until just firm and slightly pink. Garnish with lemon slices and serve with crusty bread and tossed salad.

Marie Fe DeLeon
Gilroy, California

CHICKEN ADOBO

In the Philippines garlic is used in generous quantities. The following recipe has the advantage of being low fat as well as extremely tasty. It can be used for pork as well as chicken.

4 lbs. chicken (whole or parts such as breasts or legs
        cut into serving sized pieces)
1/2 C. vinegar; white, cider, or wine
10-12 fresh garlic cloves, chopped coarsely
1/2 C. soy sauce
1/2 C. water
coarse ground black pepper, to taste

Remove chicken skin to save calories if desired. Brown chicken briefly on all sides in a large non-stick skillet. Drain off all fat. Add garlic, soy, vinegar, water and pepper. Cover and simmer for 30 minutes or until chicken is tender. Turn chicken once during cooking. Serve with rice.

Travis Reed
Capitola, California

GAME HENS WITH MUSTARD BUTTER

2 Cornish game hens (split in half)
6 Tbls. unsalted butter
4 Tbls. Sweet & Spicy Garlic Mustard
1 C. Garlic Festival Stir Fry Sauce
salt and fresh ground pepper

     Marinate hen halves overnight in Stir Fry Sauce.
Remove hens from sauce. Combine butter and
mustard and spread under the skin. Sprinkle with salt
and pepper and roast or grill until done inside and
crisp outside.

     Serves 4

Lawrence James
Dallas, Texas

GARLIC STEAKS DONATO

The unanimous winner of the Great Garlic contest in Dallas. The marinade originally was given to the family of Lawrence James by their gardener, Donato. Thus...

4-6 cloves fresh garlic, minced
1/2 C. grated Parmesan cheese
3 Tbls. butter, softened
1 Tbls. Marsala wine
1 Tbls. brandy
1 tsp. tomato paste
1/2 tsp. salt
1/2 tsp. black pepper
2 lbs. sirloin; or 4 sirloin strips or fillet mignons

Combine all ingredients except steak in food processor and blend to a paste. Grill steaks over medium coals to almost desired degree of doneness, turning once. Spread paste evenly over meat and return to grill, paste side up, until mixture begins to bubble; approximately 1-2 minutes.

Takko Machi
Garlic Festival & Sister City

MUSSELS STEAMED IN SAKE & GARLIC

3 lbs. fresh mussels, cleaned and beards removed
3 C. sake
10-15 fresh garlic cloves, minced
4 slices fresh ginger root
fresh ground black pepper
several sprigs Chinese parsley

Soak mussels in cold water for 1 hour before cooking. Drain. Place all ingredients except mussels in a large saucepan and bring to a boil. Reduce heat to medium, add mussels and cook 5-6 minutes or until mussels have opened. Remove mussels to serving bowls, ladling cooking broth over them. Discard any closed mussels. Serve with rice, Japanese cabbage or spinach salad and more sake.

Dr. Craig Kolodge
Univ. of California-Cooperative Extension

GARLIC HERB FRITTATA

This is a delicious dish for a brunch or picnic. It is best served at room temperature. For carrying to a picnic and a nice presentation try partially hollowing out a round crusty loaf of bread and sliding the frittata inside.

4 Tbls. olive oil
1 tsp. fresh garlic, minced (or Garli Garni™)
30-40 whole roasted cloves of garlic
1 each: red and yellow bell peppers, sliced thin
2 zucchini, sliced thin
1 onion, sliced thin
10-12 leaves of spinach or arugula
12 eggs
salt and pepper
1/2 C. chopped fresh herbs; oregano, thyme, basil, parsley
1/2 C. fresh grated Parmesan or Romano cheese

Heat oven to 350°. In a large oven proof skillet heat oil. Add onion and minced garlic. When onion is soft add other vegetables except spinach and cook stirring for about 5 minutes until vegetables have softened and liquid has evaporated.

Beat the eggs with salt, pepper and herbs and pour over vegetables in the skillet. Increase heat to medium-high and cook about 3 minutes just until eggs begin to set. Sprinkle whole garlic cloves evenly over the top. Arrange spinach leaves over top and sprinkle with the cheese. Place in the oven and bake about 10 minutes until eggs are set. Remove from oven and let cool slightly.

Serve from the skillet or remove to bread.

The Stinking Rose
San Francisco, California

BRAISED RABBIT

2 rabbits (cleaned and boned)
1 C. sliced mushrooms
1 C. sliced shitake mushrooms
1 C. peeled shallots
1 C. sliced onions
1/2 C. diced pancetta
1/2 C. sliced green olives
2 C. canned pear tomatoes
2 Tbls. fresh thyme
1 Tbls. fresh rosemary
1/2 C. red wine vinegar
2 C. red wine
3 C. chicken broth
garlic mashed potatoes (see Bradley Ogden's garlic
        mashed potatoes, pg. 81)

Dust rabbit with flour. Heat a sauté pan with olive oil. Brown rabbit and transfer to a roasting pan. In another sauté pan, cook pancetta until brown. Add shallots and onion. Cook for 3-4 minutes. Add mushrooms. Cook another 3-4 minutes. Add tomatoes, herbs and olives. Cook 3-4 minutes. Add red wine, reduce liquid by 1/2. Add chicken stock and vinegar. Cover rabbit with sauce and bake uncovered at 350° for 1-1/2 hours.

Serve over garlic mashed potatoes.

GRANNY IS A GARLIC GUMMER

Granny is a garlic gummer,
the family thinks her breath's a bummer.
While daily stress gets other folks,
Granny takes her garlic dose,
and remains a sea of calm despite,
the arguments and family fights.

She takes it in her tea and toast,
(she likes it in her gin the most.)
She takes it in her eggs and ham,
(and mashed it in her rhubarb jam!)

The secret is the garlic haze,
that wafts around her days and days.
Nothing seems to penetrate it,
(the army's trying to duplicate it.)

So there's a moral to this story,
I'll keep it short so's not to bore ye'
those folks in Gilroy can't be wrong,
they've preached the gospel all along:
Health and happiness don't take money-
all it takes is garlic, honey!

By Nicole Willingham

Erik Howard's Neutral Zone

Ramsey, New Jersey

In creating the Neutral Zone, Erik Howard and partner Mark, two idealistic California dreamers set out to share with northern New Jersey their diverse backgrounds and fascinations. They serve only quality certified Angus beef, it is the finest found anywhere and reminiscent of the huge Angus ranches of Eastern Washington where Erik went to college. Also transplanted is their Gilroy garlic from Erik's backyard.

The Neutral Zone
Chef Michael Rose
Ramsey, New Jersey

MESQUITE TEXAS GRILL

8 oz. steak, tri-angle or fillet mignon
2 oz. Canadian bacon
2 oz. mushrooms, sliced
4 oz. heavy cream
2 Tbls. Mesquite Grill (see sources, Garlic
      Festival® Foods)
1 tsp. butter
chopped fresh garlic
olive oil

      Marinate steak in oil, garlic and 1 Tbls. Mesquite Grill for approximately 1 hour. Charbroil steak and bacon to desired doneness. In a saucepan sauté mushrooms in 1 tsp. butter and other 1 Tbls. Mesquite Grill, add cream and reduce by 1/3. On a plate place Canadian bacon, steak on top, cover with sauce and serve with corn and potatoes.

128

The Garlic Cafe

Las Vegas, Nevada

Philosophy: "Live, love and eat garlic"

        This one-of-a-kind restaurant is the brainchild
of owner Warren Klein and a "garlaholics" dream.
Dishes can be ordered on a zero-to-five garlic force
level with some patrons asking for force 10. It also
features the city's first antipasti bar where more
than a dozen garlic laden specialties can be
sampled. The menu reflects the unique approach
of the owners; they take the food seriously but have
a garlic-good time; an attitude reflected in the
naming of their dishes: "Thai Me Up, Thai Me Down";
"Que Sera Sera--Dilla"; "Valley Girl's 'Totally Fer Sure'
Chicken"; and finally Garlic Cafe chef Vince Thein's
gift to this book: "Veal Burt and Ernie (Because
Oscar's a Grouch)".

129

VEAL BURT & ERNIE
(BECAUSE OSCAR'S A GROUCH)

3 Tbls. butter
2 Tbls. minced fresh garlic
2 Tbls. minced fresh shallots
4 oz. Glacé de Viande (veal stock)
1 lb. of 2 oz. pounded veal scallops
4 oz. crab meat
2 oz. sliced shrimp
4 oz. garlic basil béarnaise (substitute fresh basil for
        tarragon and add1 tsp. of fresh minced garlic)
flour to cover veal
2 oz. Madeira (from Europe)

Melt butter in a pan with garlic and shallots. Then dredge the veal scallops in flour to coat. Just before garlic begins to brown add the veal scallops to the pan. Turn the scallops after they change color. Add the Madeira and deglaze (burn off the alcohol with flame). When flame is out add Glacé de Viande and reduce by 1/2. Remove the veal to a plate and reduce pan juices again by 1/2. Ladle juices over veal scallops. Top with crab meat and shrimp. Cover seafood with garlic basil béarnaise and place under broiler for 1-2 minutes.

Mitch Hyde
Lynchburg, Virginia

PORK WITH GARLIC, PEPPERS & BALSAMIC VINEGAR

Yep! There's even a garlic festival in Lynchburg, Virginia; complete with Garlic Cook-off, Queen contest and eating contest. Mitch sent this recipe to the Garlic Hotline for publication. It was going to be his entry in the Garlic Cook-off. He missed their deadline, but not ours!

1 each; red, yellow, and purple (or orange) bell
        peppers, seeded and julienned
1 onion, sliced thin
5 fresh garlic cloves, minced
4 thick pork loin chops
salt and fresh ground pepper
2 Tbls. olive oil
1 tsp. each minced basil, oregano and thyme
4 Tbls. Balsamic vinegar

Salt and pepper chops. Heat oil in a large, heavy skillet. Add chops and brown on both sides until cooked through. Remove chops from skillet and keep warm. Add peppers and onion and sauté until softened, 2-3 minutes. Add garlic and herbs and sauté about 30 seconds. Add vinegar and cook until vegetables are tender but not limp. Transfer to warm plates. Top with chops and pan juice. Serve.

131

The Northwest Garlic Festival

Ocean Park, Washington

Two days of fun, excitement and garlic including a garlic peeling contest, eating contest, games, a beer garden and more. The recipes they submitted were contributed by Nanci Main and Jimella Lucas of The Ark Restaurant in Nahcaotta, Washington. At the 1988 Garlic Festival Dinner this bread was made into the shape of foot-high garlic bulbs with green onion tops, (Szechwan Brioche, pg. 92).

The following recipe was compliments of Helen & Don McDaniel, and is delicious.

The Northwest Garlic Festival
Helen and Don McDaniel
Chris and Tom Wolff
Long Beach, Washington

SQUIID STUFFED WITH GARLIC, SPINACH, FETA CHEESE & RICE

16 medium squid, cleaned (chopped tentacles may be
     used in stuffing)
1 head garlic, peeled and chopped
1 bunch spinach leaves.
     cleaned and finely chopped
4 green onions, chopped (tops included)
1/2 C. cooked short grain white rice
1/2 C. crumbled Greek Feta cheese
     (not domestic Feta)
1 tsp. white pepper
1/4 tsp. cayenne pepper
2 C. cooked Basmati rice mixed with
     2 Tbls. dried dill
1/4 C. flour mixed with 1 Tbls. sweet
     Hungarian paprika
8 sun-dried tomatoes, in olive oil
1 lemon, sliced
1/4 C. olive oil

    Sauté garlic in 2 Tbls. olive oil for 1 minute. Add
the green onions and spinach. Toss well and sauté
until spinach is wilted. Add the rice, cheese, white, and
cayenne pepper. Mix well and remove from heat.

    Stuff squid with the garlic mix. Dust the squid
with flour/paprika mix. Sauté squid in remaining olive
oil until light golden. Drain tomatoes. Arrange 4 squid
per serving on top of Basmati rice with dill. Place 2
tomatoes and 2 lemon slices on each plate. Serve.

LINGUINI WITH SCALLOPS & HERB CREAM

1 lb. linguini
1 stick butter
2-3 garlic cloves, minced
1 Tbls. basil, chopped
dash white pepper
20-25 baby scallops
1/2 C. grated Parmesan cheese
1/2 C. cream
parsley for garnish

Prepare linguini according to directions. Meanwhile, melt butter in skillet. In butter sauté garlic and basil and white pepper (to taste). To the herb butter add scallops and sauté 3-4 minutes. Toward the end add the cream and Parmesan. Stir until sauce thickens. Toss with pasta and garnish with parsley and Parmesan.

Caryl Simpson
Garlic Festival Foods
Gilroy, California

GARLIC FESTIVAL CHILI

50 medium garlic cloves
4-5 lbs. pork loin, 2 inches thick
3 onions, cut 1 inch thick
1/2 C. vegetable oil
Garli Garni™
1/4 C. paprika
2-3 Tbls. chili powder
1-1/2 Tbls. file powder
1 jalepeno chili, seeded and chopped
5 C. chicken or pork stock
2 C. pureéd tomatoes
2 dried ancho chilies, trimmed and chopped
1/4 C. flour

The day before serving:

Blanch garlic cloves in boiling water until tender,
7-10 minutes. Drain. Prepare a hot fire in barbecue
and place the rack about 4 inches from the coals.
Liberally season the pork with Garli Garni™, brush the
pork and onions with the oil and grill pork until crisp on
the outside, rare on the inside; and the onions until
charred. Cool both.
Dice the pork and onions to 1/2 inch cubes, set
aside. Heat oil in a Dutch oven or heavy, deep skillet
over medium heat until very hot. whisk in the flour and
reduce heat. Whisk until the roux is deep brown and
then cool. Combine paprika, chili powder, file, and
jalepeno in a bowl. Bring the stock , tomatoes and
anchos to a simmer in a saucepan. Place the roux over
low heat and whisk in the spices. Cook 5 minutes
stirring often. Whisk in the hot stock one cup at a time.
Add the onions and bring to a boil. Add 1-2 Tbls. Garli
Garni™. reduce heat and simmer for an hour stirring
occasionally (30-40 minutes). Add pork, trimmed of fat,
and simmer until cooked through, about 15-20 minutes.
Season with salt to taste.
Refrigerate overnight. Reheat over medium heat
before serving. Great with garlic bread!

135

Billy "Bulb" Doskocil
Grandview, Texas

GARLIC BLESSED
GAME HENS
(SMOKED)

game hens
Garli Garni™
lemon pepper

Wash hens thoroughly. Cover liberally with Garli Garni™ and lemon pepper, inside and out. Don't be shy with either ingredient.

Smoke hens in a Brinkman type smoker for 3 hours with pecan or preferred hardwood. Serve with wild rice.

LIBATIONS

Yes! You read right; Drinks!

GARTINI

2 jiggers gin
1/2 tsp. dry vermouth
1 garlic stuffed olive or 2 pickled garlic cloves for
        garnish

In a cocktail pitcher combine the gin, vermouth and 1 cup ice cubes. Stir well and strain into a cocktail glass. Garnish.

Makes one drink.

GARLI MARY

1 jigger vodka
1/2 C. tomato juice
1/2 tsp. Garli Garni™
2 tsp. fresh lemon juice
Worcestershire, to taste
Tobasco, to taste
1 lemon wedge
2 pickled garlic cloves on toothpick (or cocktail skewer)
for garnish

In a shaker combine all ingredients, except the garnish, with 1 cup ice cubes and shake well. Strain into a tall glass and garnish with pickled garlic cloves (and an optional celery stick).

Arizona Garlic Festival
Verde Valley, Arizona

ONION'S GARLIC SHOOTER

The "shooter" experience is reportedly followed by an immediate feeling of rejuvenation called the "shooter rush" and is the creation of the Onion family. Garlic legend maintains that garlic is a stimulant which gives strength and protection. Modern research has begun to identify the ingredients in garlic which help prevent disease.

1 clove garlic per person
1-2 slices lemon

Chop garlic and scoop into a cup. Squeeze lemon juice into the garlic. Add 1-2 Tbls. of water.

Important: Swirl cup to achieve a circling motion and drink in one gulp. Enjoy!

Camp Verde, Arizona

139

Louella Kisner
South Daytona, Florida

SHARI TAYLOR'S MOTHER'S GARLIC MORNING EYE OPENER

1 clove fresh garlic, minced
3 capfuls vinegar
water to fill glass
chaser: 1 Tbls. honey

This would open my eyes!!!

VEGETABLE GARLIC COCKTAIL

To any homemade or juice bar vegetable juice add a couple of cloves of fresh garlic while pressing or whole cloves as a garnish.

The Cincinnati Garlic Festival

Cincinnati, Ohio

The Cincinnati Garlic Festival is held in Cincinnati's historic district "Over the Rhine". Because of the area's predominant German heritage, garlic sausage is a main feature of this festival. It also includes a queen pageant, eating contest, and garlic beer.

Cincinnati Garlic Festival
Cincinnati, Ohio

CINCINNATI GARLIC SHOOTER

In large shot glass:

1 fresh shucked oyster
1 shot vodka
1 clove garlic, minced
catsup
pinch of fresh horseradish
dash of Worcestershire
salt and pepper, to taste
squeeze of lemon

Mix all ingredients and drink. When shaking subsides, resume life.

FID-AULX
(fid-o)

Dogs like garlic too!

FID-AULX
(AULX: ARCHAIC (OLD) FRENCH FOR GARLIC)

Yes, dogs like garlic too! Look at the ingredients on most commercial pet foods and you'll find garlic listed as an ingredient. And garlic is good for them, just as it's good for their humans.

Putting a clove or two of raw garlic in your dog's food will keep him/her flea free. Usually you have to mince it and sneak it into their food. Some dogs will eat anything their human feeds them. Such is the case with our dog, Murphy. He'll eat raw cloves and positively loves roasted garlic. This works for cats too.

The following is a garlicky treat you can make at home for your canine (or feline) best friend. They're nutritious, pets love them and they help with the flea problem.

Heather Simpson
Gilroy, California

HEATHER'S GARLICKY
DOG BISCUITS

1 C. white flour
1 C. whole wheat flour
1/2 C. wheat germ
1/2 C. powdered milk
1/2 tsp. salt
1-2 Tbls. liver powder (available at health food stores)
1 tsp. brown sugar
6 Tbls. vegetable oil
1 egg, beaten
1/2 C. water
10 large garlic cloves, finely minced

Heat oven to 325°. Combine dry ingredients. Mix
and add oil and egg. Add water to make a stiff dough.
Knead until pliable. Roll out on floured surface 1/4 to
1/2 inch thick. Cut out with cookie cutters or biscuit
cutter. Bake for 20-25 minutes. Use bone, cat or people
shaped cutters.

During holidays when you're making cookies for
friends and relatives these are fun and different to add
as gifts for your friend's pets.

SOURCES

1. The Garlic Hotline

A newsletter of garlicky news, recipes, and information on garlic festivals and events throughout the world.

P.O. Box 2303
Gilroy, California 95021
1 800 4-GARLIX

2. Garli Garni™

The best all-purpose garlic seasoning in the world. Featured on Good Morning America, the Home Show and in busy kitchens everywhere. Also: Sweet & Spicy Garlic Mustard, Picked Garlic, Garlic Salsa, Garlic Festival Stir Fry, and fresh garlic. A full line of Gourmet Gold and Garlic Festival food products and gifts

Garlic Festival Foods®
P.O. Box 1145
Gilroy, California 95021
1 800 4-GARLIX

3. Dried Tomatoes

Timber Crest Farms
4791 Dry Creek Road
Healdsburg, California 95448
(707) 433-8251

Compiled by "Huck" Hagenbuch

GARLIC: FACT & FANCY

Chic. Reek. Garlique. It all rhymes, and hundreds of writers have waxed eloquent about the stinking rose, as garlic has come to be known. It is the stuff of which legends are made: myth transcends reality, and reality becomes ever more intriguing as new characteristics of garlic are discovered.

In garlic country, there isn't a home in which hangs a garlic braid that cannot attest to the ability to ward off vampires. In fact, there hasn't been a report of a vampire attack in the written history of Gilroy, "garlic capital" of the world.

Garlic is the serious subject of numerous world-wide scientific investigations, many of which validate and reinforce the medicinal and nutritional value of garlic in a regimen of health. For example, it has been reported that garlic can reduce fat levels in the blood, as well as aid dissolution of blood clots, which may prove helpful to potential heart attack and stroke victims. Some reports conclude that garlic can prove effective in combating cancer and fungus infections.

As science learns ever more about the contribution of good nutrition to long and healthy lives, it finds that garlic is a growing factor in the well-being of healthy individuals. Folk-lore tends to be reaffirmed every day.

Today, studies have verified that in areas of China and Italy in which garlic is a major nutritional element, stomach cancer seems to occur at a much lower rate than in those in which garlic consumption is much less.

So the folklore prevails, but science is making it more factual every day. In fact, lives in which garlic plays a major role seem to be happier, healthier lives, enjoying life longer. One look around the garlic festivals everywhere tends to confirm all of these factors, as young and old alike join together in tribute to and celebration of the "Stinking Rose".

To order additional copies:

International Garlic Festival Cookbook

P.O. Box 1145
Gilroy, CA. 95021

or call: 1 (800) 4-GARLIX

$9.95 per copy

Receive a 10% discount when ordering 10 cookbooks.

Receive a 20% discount when ordering more than 10 books.

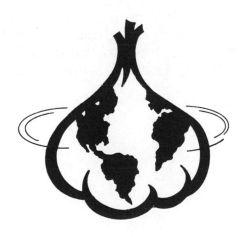

ABOUT THE AUTHOR

Caryl Simpson is the president of Garlic Festival® Foods and the creator of an extensive line of gourmet food products and cook booklets. Billed by the media as the "High Priestess of the Garlic Cult" she was the first person to take the pungent herb for which Gilroy was already famous and whip it into some heady concoctions. These can now be purchased throughout the United States and elsewhere under the Garlic Festival & Gourmet Gold Labels.

The mother of two adult children, Heather & Ted, her interest in the food industry grew out of a love of traveling the world, gardening, cooking and entertaining. Eventually, a career as an artist and owner of an advertising agency evolved into a full time career in the food business; what she calls "a harmonic convergence" of her favorite things.

Caryl currently lives and works in Gilroy, California, "The Garlic Capital of the World", with her partner Tom. Caryl and daughter Heather, have recently added a new phase to the business with the opening of the Garlic Festival Store & Gallery located in downtown Gilroy.

Garlic Festivals mentioned throughout this book

Also mentioned are two of Gilroy's sister cities which also host garlic festivals. They are Takko Machi, Japan (chicken wings) and Monticelli di Ongina in Italy. (Died and gone to Monticelli) There are many other garlic festivals throughout the world and new ones cropping up every year; ample proof of garlic's magic.